# Look

COMBO SPLIT 4A

CB079265


STUDENT'S BOOK AUTHOR

Rob Sved

WORKBOOK AUTHORS

Fiona Beddall

Teresa Bestwick

COURSE CONSULTANTS

Paul Dummett

Elaine Boyd



NATIONAL GEOGRAPHIC LEARNING

Australia • Brazil • Mexico • Singapore • United Kingdom • United States

COMBO SPLIT 4A

# Contents

COMBO SPLIT 4B

# Contents

Camping in the evening, Borneo, Indonesia

# Look and remember

LESSON 1

**1** Look at the photo. Tick (✓) the words you can see.

| | | | |
|---|---|---|---|
| moon | ☐ | stars | ☐ |
| forest | ☐ | building | ☐ |
| picnic | ☐ | museum | ☐ |
| tent | ☐ | friends | ☐ |
| bat | ☐ | tree | ☐ |
| cloud | ☐ | skyscraper | ☐ |

**2** Read and complete the postcard.

Hi,

How are you? I'm 1 *camping / camp* with my friends again this year. We always 2 *coming / come* to this beautiful place. There 3 *are / aren't* many people so it's calm and quiet. At the moment, we're 4 *eating / eat* outside. We're having 5 *a / some* pasta and salad. Tomorrow we're going 6 *go / to go* canoeing and then we want to climb some trees in the forest.

See you soon!

**3** Answer the questions. Then compare your answers in small groups.

**1** Would you like to go camping here? Why? / Why not?

**2** How often do you go camping?

**3** What other activities do you like doing outside?

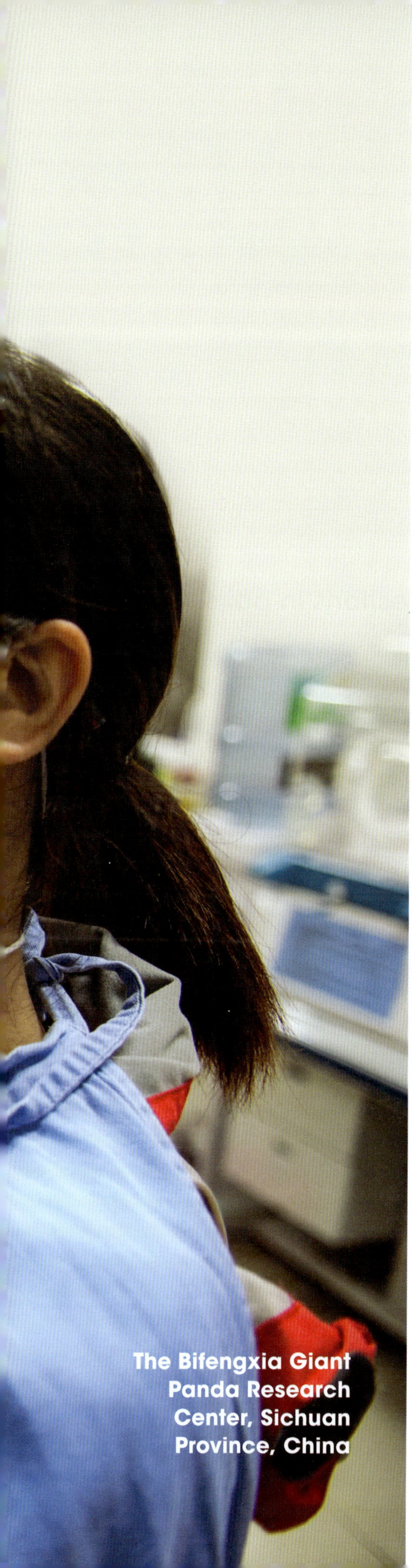

The Bifengxia Giant Panda Research Center, Sichuan Province, China

# Look and remember

LESSON 2

**1** Look at the photo. Read and write T (true) or F (false).

1 There are two people in the photo.
2 The woman is wearing glasses.
3 The woman is angry.
4 The man is looking at the panda.
5 The man has got short hair.

**2** Listen. Complete the information about giant pandas. TR: 1

## Giant Pandas

**Number in China:** [1]_______________ giant pandas

**Size at birth:** [2]_______________ centimetres long

**Size of adults:** taller than [3]_______________ metre

**Food:** bamboo, for [4]_______________ hours every day

**Age:** up to [5]_______________ years old

**3** Work in pairs. Choose another wild animal and write a factfile.

**Animal:** _______________

Country/Countries: _______________

How many: _______________

Size: _______________

Food: _______________

How long they live: _______________

**4** Work with another pair. Ask and answer questions to guess each other's animal.

What does it eat?

It eats small animals.

LESSON 3

# Look and remember

## 1 Write the odd one out.

| | | | | | |
|---|---|---|---|---|---|
| 1 | lake | river | waterfall | village | ______ |
| 2 | pasta | bottle | plate | cup | ______ |
| 3 | ant | dolphin | kangaroo | panda | ______ |
| 4 | curly | straight | moustache | long | ______ |
| 5 | neck | cough | shoulder | stomach | ______ |
| 6 | son | daughter | sister | grandmother | ______ |

## 2 Write two odd-one-out puzzles for your friend.

1 ______ ______ ______ ______

2 ______ ______ ______ ______

## 3 Write questions. Then ask and answer the questions in pairs.

1 are / you / old / how

______________________________?

2 your / is / when / birthday

______________________________?

3 and sisters / got / brothers / any / you / have

______________________________?

4 Saturdays / you / do / on / what / usually / do

______________________________?

5 like / books / you / do / comic / reading

______________________________?

6 on Sunday / going to / you / what / do / are

______________________________?

## 4 Think about your favourite things. Then ask and answer in small groups.

animal sport food place to visit country activity fruit

What's your favourite animal?

A cat. What's yours?

UNIT 1

# All kinds of jobs

Burj Khalifa, Dubai

**Look at the photo. Answer the questions.**

1 Where is the man?

2 What is he doing? Why?

3 What does he need for his job?

4 Would you like this job? Why? / Why not?

LESSON 1
# Words

## 1 Listen and repeat. TR: 2

actor

clown

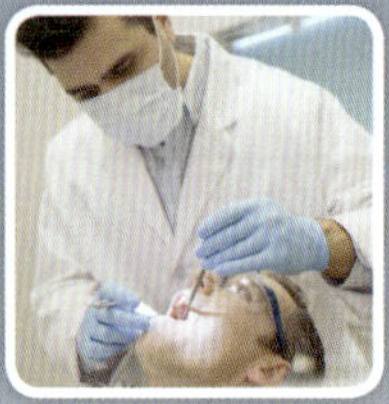
dentist

firefighter

nurse

photographer

pilot

police officer

waiter

## 2 Answer the questions.

1 Which jobs do people sometimes do outside?
2 Which jobs help other people?

## 3 Listen to the conversation about smoke jumpers. Write T (true) or F (false). TR: 3

1 Smoke jumpers jump out of a plane as a hobby. ☐
2 A smoke jumper is a kind of firefighter. ☐
3 Smoke jumpers fight fires in forests all year. ☐
4 The smoke jumpers carry all the equipment when they jump. ☐
5 The smoke jumper in the photo is Russian. ☐
6 There are about 400 US smoke jumpers. ☐

Smoke jumpers are training in the US.

# Grammar

LESSON 2

## 1 Listen and read. TR: 4

**Present simple and present continuous**

We use the present simple for things that we do all the time or that we do many times. We often use it with time expressions like *every day, on Mondays, once a week*.

*They **fight** fires in forests **every summer**.*

We use the present continuous to talk about things that are happening now. We often use it with time expressions like *now, at the moment, today*.

*They **aren't fighting** a fire **today**. They**'re training**.*

## 2 Complete the text with the verbs in brackets. Use the present simple or continuous.

My mum is a police officer. She [1]__________ (work) at a police station in Seoul. She [2]__________ (drive) a police car every day. From Monday to Friday, she [3]__________ (eat) her lunch at work. Police officers in Korea [4]__________ (work) at the weekend and at night too.

Today, my mum [5]__________ (do) something different. She [6]__________ (visit) a primary school and she [7]__________ (talk) to the children about her job. The children [8]__________ (ask) questions about her badges and her radio.

## 3 Work in pairs. Ask and answer.

1 What / wear / school / every / day?
2 What / do / at the weekend?
3 What / your teacher / do / right now?
4 Have breakfast / at the moment?

What do you wear at school every day?

I wear jeans and a T-shirt every day.

LESSON 3 # Reading

**1** Look at the photo. What is the man doing?

**2** What is the film *Walking With Giants* about? Listen and read. TR: 5

## Walking With Giants

Hans Weise is a **film director**. He makes many different kinds of films. He likes making **animations**. There aren't usually any actors in these films. Hans uses **models** instead. He works with a **designer** Fernando Baptista to make models of the people, places and objects. Fernando paints the models and then Hans takes photos of them. After he takes a photo, he moves the models. Then he takes another photo. At the end, he puts all the photos together to make a film. This is called 'stop-motion animation'.

*Walking With Giants* is about the statues on Easter Island, a small island in the middle of the Pacific Ocean. The statues are very big and heavy. How did they get there? No one knows for sure, but there are different ideas. Hans and Fernando make animations with models to show these ideas. One idea is that people moved the statues there a long time ago. Hans and Fernando use toy dolls as models of the people. *Walking With Giants* is about four minutes long, but it was four weeks' work!

**3** Match the words in bold in the text with their meanings.

1 a small copy of something
2 a film people make with drawings or models
3 a person who draws how to make something
4 a person who makes a film

**4** Read again. Answer the questions.

1 Who paints the models?
2 What does Hans do before he takes a photo?
3 Why did Hans and Fernando make this film?
4 How long is the film?
5 Would you like to be a film director or a designer? Why?

Moai statues on Easter Island, Chile

# Grammar

LESSON 4

## 1 Listen and read. TR: 6

**Adverbs of frequency**

We use adverbs of frequency to show how often we do things.

*always*
*usually*
*often*
*sometimes*
*rarely*
*never*

We use them before verbs in the present simple, but after the verb *to be*.

*The designer **often** makes two or three models.*

*They are **usually** difficult to paint.*

## 2 Put the adverbs of frequency in Hans Weise's description.

1 I use toys for people and animals. (sometimes)
2 I put the camera on a table. (always) I hold it in my hand, because it can move. (never)
3 I take a picture of the models, move them a bit and then take another picture. (usually)
4 I take five pictures for each one second of film. (usually) Then I put the pictures on my computer.
5 I have hundreds of pictures. (often) I make the animation with a computer program.
6 It's easy to make animated films, but they are very long. (rarely)

## 3 Work in groups. Say true or false sentences about your day. Can your partners guess?

I always get up before seven o'clock.

That's true.

False!

# LESSON 5 Song

**1** Listen and read. What are the jobs? TR: 7

## Different jobs

I'm in the field.
I'm cutting fields of wheat.
I love my job, I work outside,
I grow the food we eat.

*Chorus*
*Different jobs for different people.*
*What's my job? Can you guess?*

I'm on the plane.
I'm flying through the sky.
I love my job, I travel a lot
To Paris and Mumbai.
*Chorus*

I'm in the café.
I'm carrying food around.
I love my job, I meet new people
From many different towns.
*Chorus*

I'm in the class.
I'm teaching maths today.
I love my job, the children learn
And I learn a lot from them!
*Chorus*

**VALUE** Be curious.
*Workbook, Lesson 6*

**2** Listen and sing. TR: 8 and 9

**3** Sing and act. TR: 10

# Writing An interview

LESSON 6

**1** **Read the interview. What is Kobie's job?**

## An interview with
# Kobie Boykins

**Where do you work, Kobie?**

I work at NASA in California. NASA is the USA's space agency.

**What's your job?**

I'm an engineer. I make robots.

**Where do your robots go?**

They go into space and to other planets, like Mars.

**Do you like your job?**

Yes, I do. I love it! It's amazing to think that *my* robots are travelling in space at the moment.

**What is your favourite robot?**

My first robot, called the Sojourner Rover. It was the first robot to go to Mars. It had three cameras on it for taking photos.

**What are you working on at the moment?**

I'm making a new robot for the next trip to Mars. It has 23 cameras and an arm to pick things up.

**2** **Read. Then look at the interview again and answer the questions.**

When we do an **interview**, we usually follow these steps:

- First, we think about the information we want to know.
- Then, we write some questions.
- Finally, we ask the questions and write the answers.

Which questions are about

1 Kobie's job?
2 how Kobie feels?
3 what Kobie is doing at the moment?
4 Kobie's favourite things?

**3** **Writing skill** Interview questions

a **Write three questions for an interview about someone's school.**

1 Where / go / school?

_______________

2 What / favourite / subject?

_______________

3 What / learn / about / at the moment?

_______________

_______________

b **Work in pairs. Ask and answer the questions.**

**4** **Interview someone in your family about his/her job. First, write your questions.**

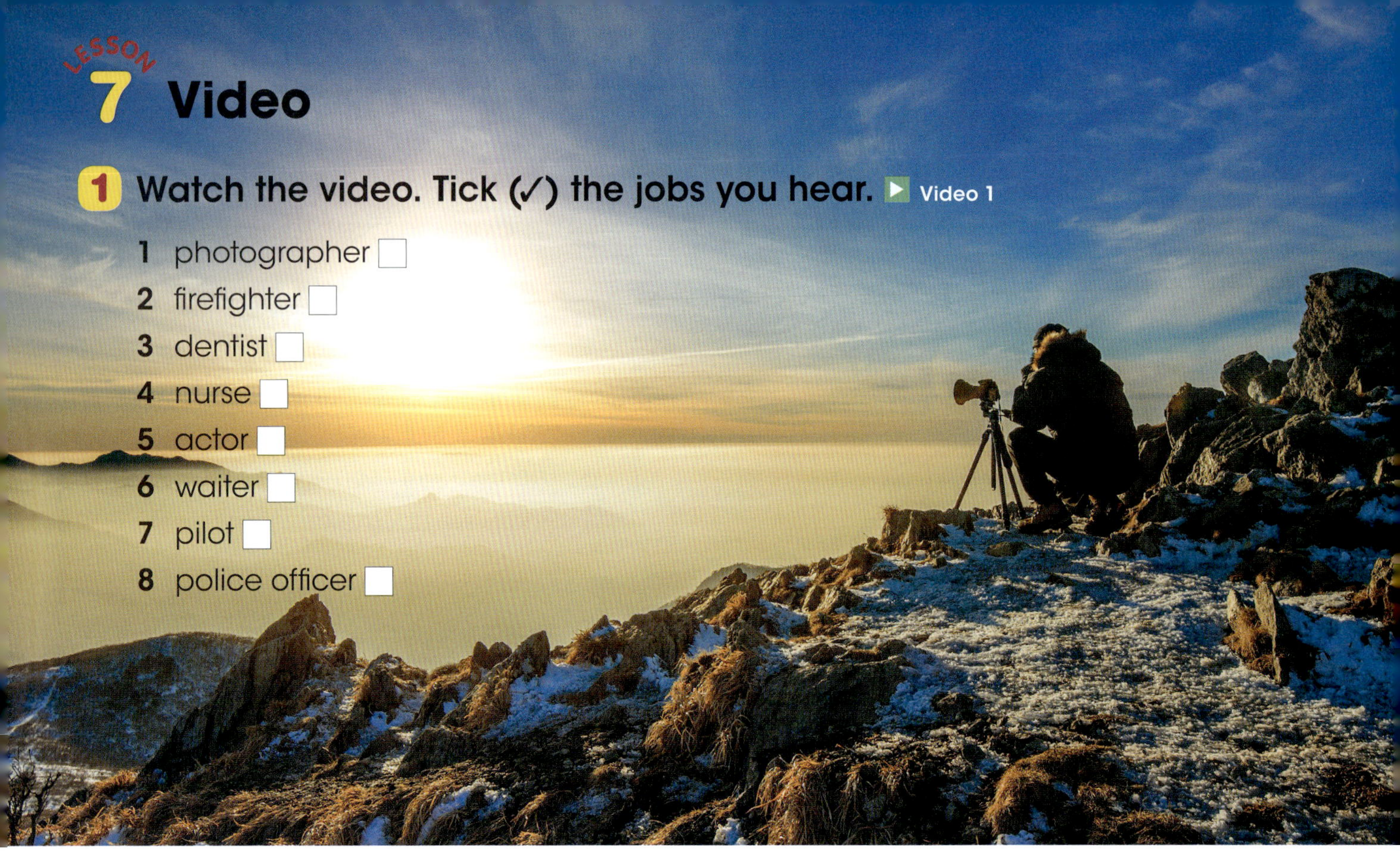

# LESSON 7 Video

## 1 Watch the video. Tick (✓) the jobs you hear. ▶ Video 1

1 photographer ☐
2 firefighter ☐
3 dentist ☐
4 nurse ☐
5 actor ☐
6 waiter ☐
7 pilot ☐
8 police officer ☐

## 2 Watch the video again. Match the children with two things that they talk about. ▶ Video 1

1 AJ C ☐  2 Rhiane ☐ ☐  3 Lara ☐ ☐

A working in a team
B taking photos of trees
C taking things to villages
D protecting people and forests
E flying over forests
F swimming in the sea

## 3 Read and write T (true) or F (false).

1 AJ's uncle works in Alaska.
2 There are many forests where AJ's uncle works.
3 Rhiane wants to be a dentist.
4 Rhiane wants to travel when she is older.
5 Lara's dad and grandpa were firefighters.
6 Lara thinks a firefighter has a difficult job.

## 4 Work in pairs. Discuss the questions.

1 Which of the jobs mentioned in the video do you want to do? Why?
2 Talk about a job someone in your family does.
3 How can you choose the best job for you? What do you have to think about?

# Move to the music!

UNIT 2

Ice Music Festival in Geilo, Norway

**Look at the photo. Answer the questions.**

1 What is the woman doing?
2 What is the harp made of?
3 What is she wearing? Why?
4 What musical instruments can you play?

LESSON 1

# Words

## 1 Listen and repeat. TR: 11

cello

classical music

concert

dancer

drums

flute

keyboard

pop music

singer

violin

## 2 Complete the text with the words from Exercise 1.

Orchestras are groups of musicians. They give 1 ________ in theatres. They usually play 2 ________ music, but they sometimes play 3 ________ music too. The musicians play different instruments like the 4 v________, the 5 c________, the 6 f________ or the 7 d________. But they don't usually play electric instruments like the 8 ________. A 9 ________ sometimes sings a song, but there aren't any 10 ________s.

3 Listen to the presentation about the Recycled Orchestra of Cateura. Circle the correct answer. TR: 12

1 The orchestra is from *Paraguay / Colombia* in South America.
2 Favio Chavez started the orchestra in *2006 / 2012*.
3 They made instruments from old *cars / tins*.
4 There were music classes every *day / week*.
5 They played their first concert in a different country in *2012 / 2020*.
6 They played in *Brazil / Mexico*.

# Grammar LESSON 2

1 Read and listen. TR: 13

**Past simple: *be***
*It was their first concert.*
*It wasn't easy.*
*Were the instruments expensive?*
*Yes, they were. / No, they weren't.*
**Past simple: regular verbs**
*In 2012, they visited Brazil.*
*The children didn't play instruments then.*
*Did you guess? Yes, I did. / No, I didn't.*

2 Complete the text with these verbs. Use the past simple.

clap be (x2) play love watch visit

This month, we [1]______________ many concerts with an American rock band called Metallica. More than 35,000 people [2]______________ us at the first concert. We [3]______________ very nervous. But the audience [4]______________ the concert and they [5]______________ a lot. We [6]______________ six different countries in South America. It [7]______________ an amazing experience!

3 Make sentences in the past simple.

1 Children / not clean / their instruments
2 Favio Chavez / not be / a farmer
3 They / use / paint tins to make instruments
4 It / not be / easy to make the instruments
5 In 2014 / the orchestra / not visit / Europe

4 Think of three things you did yesterday. Ask your partner.

Did you walk to school yesterday?

No, I didn't.

LESSON 3 **Reading**

**1** Look at the photo. What are they doing?

**2** Listen and read. TR: 14

# INDIAN
## music and dance

My name is Soumik Datta. My brother, Souvid, is a photographer. We live in England, but we were born in India. We wanted to learn more about dance and music in India, and we wanted to make a film. So, in 2015, we visited India and saw more than 100 different musicians.

One group of musicians from Karnataka are famous for their dance called 'the Kunitha'. They wear colourful costumes and many of them play the drums. They sing and jump too. All the men are farmers, but they love dancing.

We filmed their show. It was incredible! The dancers **carried** big drums and they **banged** them loudly. They all **shouted** and they kicked their feet. Then they played their drums quietly and some of the dancers **climbed** onto the drums to make a tower. Then they banged their drums quickly. It was very exciting.

You can watch these dancers playing their drums in one of our programmes. We hope you enjoy it!

**3** Read again. What did Soumik and Souvid see? Circle the correct answer.

1 The dancers *carried / kicked* thei drums to the field.
2 They *jumped / climbed* high in the air and *banged / kicked* their feet.
3 Then the dancers *banged / kicked* their drums loudly and *shouted / climbed* loudly too.
4 Some dancers *climbed / carried* onto the drums.

**4** Read again. Correct the sentences.

1 Soumik's brother is a musician.
2 The dancers are all doctors.
3 They always play their drums loudly.
4 The show was boring.

Dancers in Karnataka, India

# Grammar

LESSON 4

## 1 Listen and read. TR: 15

**Adverbs of manner**

We use adverbs of manner to describe how we do things. They usually go at the end of a sentence.

*They played quietly.*

*They banged the drums loudly.*

An important irregular adverb is *good* → *well.*

*They played well.*

## 2 Complete the text with the adverbs of the words in brackets.

There are many different kinds of drums. The musicians from Karnataka carry big drums and they play them 1 *loudly* (loud). They play them very 2__________ (good) too! The Orquesta de Cateura have big drums on the floor. They sometimes play them 3__________ (slow) and sometimes they play them 4__________ (quick). Pop groups use drums as well. When they play slow songs, they sometimes play them 5__________ (quiet). Drummers need to listen 6__________ (careful) to the rhythm.

## 3 Answer the questions about you.

How do you …

**1** eat your breakfast every morning?

**2** walk to school?

**3** talk to your friends?

**4** work in class?

**5** do your English homework?

How do you eat your breakfast every morning?

I eat it quickly!

LESSON 5 **Song**

**1** **Listen and read. How do you dance?** TR: 16

## At the dance!

Some people danced slowly.
They moved their arms up and down.
Some people danced quickly.
They hopped and jumped around.

*Chorus*
*But no one danced badly.*
*We danced! We danced! We danced!*

Some people danced sadly.
They looked down at the floor.
Some people danced happily.
They smiled and danced some more.
*Chorus*

Some people danced carefully.
They all moved in a square.
Some people danced wildly.
They jumped high in the air.
*Chorus*

Some people danced quietly.
Their moves were very neat.
Some people danced loudly.
They shouted and stamped their feet.
*Chorus*

**2** **Listen and sing.** TR: 17 and 18

**3** **Listen and act.** TR: 19

**VALUE** **Be yourself.** *Workbook, Lesson 6*

**Guelaguetza festival, Oaxaca, Mexico**

# Writing A review

**1** **Read the review. Did Nick like the show?**

**2** **Read. Then look at Nick's review again and answer the questions.**

A **review** gives information about an event, e.g. a show, film or a book. It usually:

- says what the event was.
- says when the event was.
- describes the good things and explain why they were good.
- describes the bad things too.

1 What is the review about?
2 When did Nick see the show?
3 What did he like?
4 What bad things does he write about?

**A review of *Annie*** by Nick

Last night, we went to a theatre in New York to see a musical called *Annie*. It's about the adventures of an 11-year-old girl. She's looking for her parents. Some of the story is sad, but it has a happy ending! There's a lot of singing and dancing.

I loved the musical because the songs were great. The actors were very good singers and they danced very well too! There was a big orchestra and it played loudly. There were flutes, violins, cellos and drums. I liked the flutes because they played beautifully in the slow songs. At the end, I clapped for a long time. I didn't want it to end because I loved it so much!

**3** **Writing skill** *because*

**a Read. Then look at Nick's review again and complete the sentences.**

We use *because* to explain why we like or don't like something.

1 Nick liked the musical *because* ______________________________.

2 Nick liked the flutes ______________________________.

**b Match.**

1 I liked the costumes because
2 The drummer was great because
3 I liked the actors because
4 I didn't like the end because

A she played about ten different kinds of drum!
B they were very funny.
C it was very sad.
D they were beautiful colours.

**4** **Write a review of a show you saw at school or at a theatre.**

# LESSON 7 Video

**1 Watch the video. Match the countries (1–3) with the instruments (A–C).** Video 2

1 India ☐ 2 Spain ☐ 3 Scotland ☐

A

B

C

## 2 Watch the video again. Complete the definitions with the words. Video 2

chord loud popular stick traditional

1 When many people like something, we say it is a ______________ thing.
2 A short, thin piece of wood is a ______________ .
3 Three or more musical notes played at the same time is a ______________ .
4 When people in a place do something for many years, we say it is a ______________ thing.
5 The opposite of *quiet* is ______________ .

## 3 Circle the correct answer.

1 The sitar is usually *more than / less than* a metre long.
2 People use *a pick / their hands and fingers* to play the tabla.
3 Flamenco is typical in the *south / north* of Spain.
4 Flamenco dancers use their *arms / shoes* to make loud sounds.
5 To play the bagpipes, you *blow into / hit* the pipe.
6 You use your *arms / legs* to play the bagpipes.

## 4 Work in pairs. Discuss the questions.

1 What traditional instruments are there in your country? How do you play them?
2 What instruments do your friends and family play?
3 Which instrument would you like to learn? Why?

| | |
|---|---|
| **Where** is your house? | **Turn right** (at the supermarket). |
| **Go straight on**. | The school is **on the right**. |
| **Turn left** (at the end of the road). | |

## 1 Listen and complete the dialogue. TR: 20

**Min:** Hi, Leo.

**Leo:** Hi, Min. Where are you? It's late.

**Min:** I'm lost! Can you help me?

**Leo:** OK. Where are you now?

**Min:** I'm on Green Street, near High Street.

**Leo:** OK. Go straight on down Green Street and [1]____________ at the bookshop.

**Min:** And then?

**Leo:** Then [2]____________ and my house is [3]____________. It's number 26.

**Min:** OK. Thanks, Leo. See you soon.

**Leo:** Yes. See you soon.

## 2 Listen, check and repeat. TR: 21

## 3 Read the dialogue again and look at the map. What colour is Leo's house?

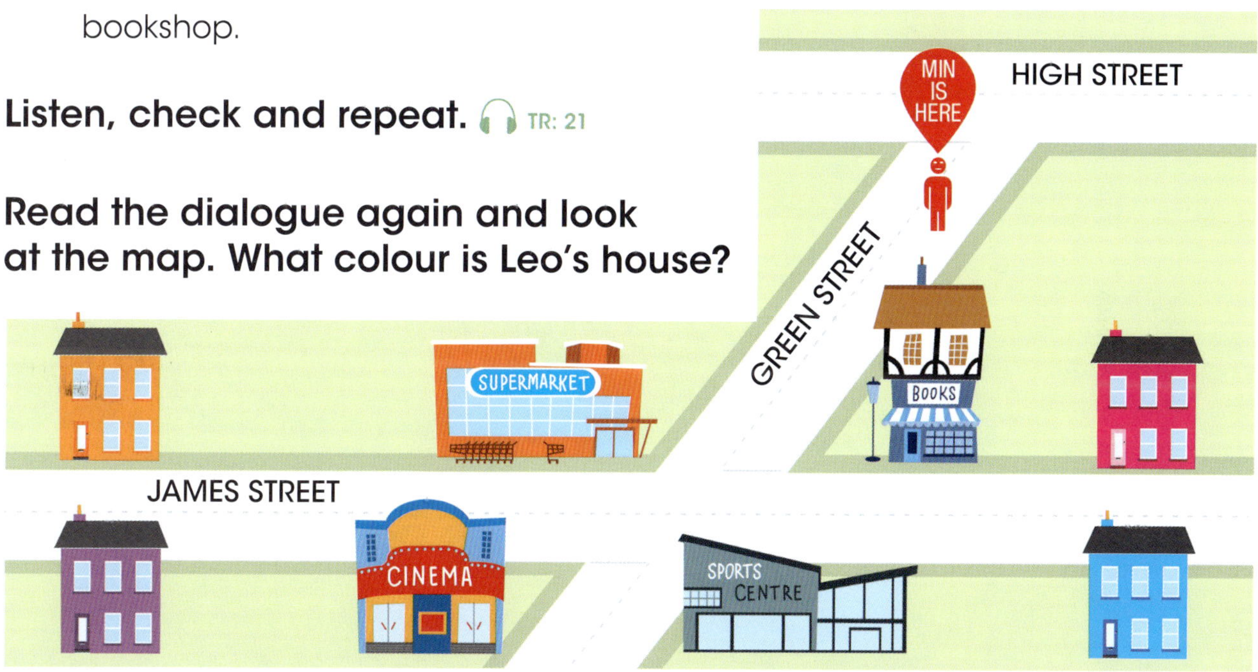


## 4 Play a game. Think of a place in your school. In pairs, give directions to your partner. Can your partner find the place?

Go out of the classroom. Turn left. Then go straight on. At the end, turn right ... Where are you?

At the café!

# Redwood forests

You're going to watch wildlife photographer, Michael 'Nick' Nichols in action. He's taking photos of the animals and trees in a redwood forest on the west coast of the US. Redwoods are huge trees. Many of the trees are more than 1,500 years old. They're the tallest trees in the world and their trunks can be nine metres thick! They can grow to more than 100 metres tall so it's difficult to take photos of them. Nick needs to find some special ways to do it.

**1 Read about redwood trees. Answer the questions.**

1 How old are the oldest redwood trees?

2 Why is it difficult to take photos of redwood trees?

**2 Watch the video. Put the sentences in order (1–5).** Video 3

- ☐ **A** Nick takes some great photos of the owls.
- ☐ **B** Nick sends a camera up the tree.
- ☐ **C** Nick gives the owls food.
- ☐ **D** The photos of the tree go into Nick's computer.
- ☐ **E** Nick puts on a costume.

Scientists studying a very tall redwood tree

**3 PROJECT Work in pairs. Make a size chart.**

Draw a chart to show the size of a redwood tree. Compare it with other trees, animals and things.

**4 Tell the class about your chart.**

A redwood tree is 100 metres tall. It's taller than the Statue of Liberty in New York, but it's shorter than the Eiffel Tower in Paris.

# Review 1: Units 1–2

## 1 Complete the text with these words. There are three words you don't need.

actor carry climb concerts dancer dentist drums pilot

When I'm older, I want to learn how to fly a plane. Maybe I can be a [1]__________ one day. I love music too. I like going to [2]__________ at my school. I go to dance classes, but I don't want to be a [3]__________ . I always [4]__________ a camera with me. My sister plays the [5]__________ and I like taking photos of her. So maybe I can be a photographer. I don't need to decide now!

## 2 Choose the best title for the text in Exercise 1.

The right job for me ☐ My sister's hobby ☐ How to fly a plane ☐

## 3 Write sentences about you.

always usually often sometimes rarely never

1 On my birthday, ____________________ .
2 At school, ____________________ .
3 ____________________ in the summer.
4 At the weekend, ____________________ .
5 When I'm happy/bored, ____________________ .

## 4 Make sentences and questions. Use the past simple.

1 she / play / the violin / at the school concert
2 they / not visit / London / yesterday
3 you / climb / up the mountain?
4 we / carry / the drums / onto the stage
5 be / keyboard / expensive?

## 5 Complete the sentences with the adverbs of the words in brackets.

1 The woman played the piano __________ . (quiet)
2 The audience clapped __________ . (loud)
3 The girl danced very __________ . (good)
4 He didn't walk to the concert __________ . (quick)
5 They played their instruments __________ . (careful)

UNIT 3

# Let's celebrate!

Mercantia, a street art festival in Certaldo, Italy

**Look at the photo. Answer the questions.**

1 What are the people looking at?

2 What other things do you think they can see in this festival?

3 What celebrations do you have in your area?

LESSON

# 1 Words

## 1 Listen and repeat. TR: 22

eat traditional food

give presents

make special food

play party games

put up decorations

see a parade

throw streamers

wear a costume

## 2 Answer the questions.

1 Which of these things do you do for / at a party?

2 Which of these things do you do at a street festival?

3 Which do you do at both?

## 3 Listen to the presentation about a harvest festival in South Korea. Circle the correct answer. TR: 23

1 Do people usually celebrate the harvest at the end of autumn? *Yes, they do. / No, they don't.*

2 Did people put up decorations for Chuseok? *Yes, they did. / No, they didn't.*

3 Did they give presents? *Yes, they did. / No, they didn't.*

4 Did people throw streamers in the parade? *Yes, they did. / No, they didn't.*

5 Did people wear traditional costumes? *Yes, they did. / No, they didn't.*

Parade to celebrate Chuseok in Seoul, South Korea with girls and women wearing traditional 'hanbok' dresses



# Grammar

## 1 Listen and read. TR: 24

**Past simple: irregular verbs**

*We **ate** traditional food.*

*They **didn't eat** pizza.*

***Did** people **wear** costumes?*

***Yes**, they **did**. / **No**, they **didn't**.*

| | | |
|---|---|---|
| eat – ate | have – had | see – saw |
| give – gave | make – made | throw – threw |
| go – went | put – put | wear – wore |

## 2 Complete the text with the verbs in brackets. Use the past simple.

Last weekend, I was at the Apple Harvest Festival, here in Pennsylvania, US. We [1]______________ (make) twenty apple pies before the festival. We [2]______________ (go) to the festival early and I [3]______________ (put up) decorations with my family. We [4]______________ (eat) many different kinds of food. My favourite was the toffee apples! The festival is really big. I [5]______________ (not / see) all of it. But I [6]______________ (see) lots of my friends there and we [7]______________ (dance) to the music together.

## 3 Make questions to ask your friend about a festival.

dance eat give make play put up see throw wear

## 4 Ask your questions from Exercise 3.

Did you dance at your party?

No, I didn't. But I listened to the music.

LESSON 3 Reading

**1** Look at the photo of a festival in Italy. Which of the chocolates would you like to try?

**2** Listen and read. TR: 25

# Wonderful food festivals in Italy

## Mica

**Where did you go?**

We went to Florence in May. We went to the Ice Cream Festival!

**What did you do?**

The festival was in a big square on a hill. We **bought** a ticket and walked around the festival. We ate many different flavours of ice cream. One was milk, honey and rice flavour, but my favourite was orange, lemon and mint. People **chose** their favourite ice cream flavour to see who was the best ice cream maker. At the end of the festival, we **took** photos with the ice cream makers!

## Anna

**Where did you go?**

We went to Perugia in October. We went to the Chocolate Festival!

**What did you do?**

On the first day, we watched people on the street. They made sculptures from huge pieces of chocolate. They were beautiful, and we ate some of the chocolate too! At the Chocolate Museum, we **learnt** about how people make chocolate. The next day, we **drank** some delicious hot chocolate.

**3** Read again. Write T (true) or F (false).

1 The Ice Cream Festival is in October. ☐
2 Mica liked the milk, honey and rice flavour more than the orange, lemon and mint flavour. ☐
3 There was a competition for the best ice cream. ☐
4 The Chocolate Festival is in Perugia. ☐
5 At the museum, Anna learnt how to make sculptures. ☐
6 Anna didn't like the hot chocolate. ☐

## Grammar

LESSON 4

4 Find the past simple of these verbs in the text.

1 buy
2 choose
3 drink
4 learn
5 take

1 Listen and read. TR: 26

**Past simple: *Wh-* questions**

*Where did you go?*

*We went to Florence.*

*What did you eat?*

*We ate ice cream.*

**Past simple: *Wh-* questions with *be***

*What was your favourite flavour?*

*Strawberry was my favourite!*

2 Put the questions in order. Look at the text on page 32 again and write the answers.

1 did / where / go / Mica

______________________________?

______________________________

2 did / buy / he / what

______________________________?

______________________________

3 did / Perugia / Anna / when / go / to

______________________________?

______________________________

4 make / what / people / from chocolate pieces / did

______________________________?

______________________________

5 eat / Anna / did / what

______________________________?

______________________________

3 Think about a festival or a celebration you went to. Ask and answer questions.

What ...? Where ...? When ...? Why ...?

be drink eat go make see wear

LESSON 5

# Song

**1** **Listen and read. Do you have street parties? What other celebrations do you have with your neighbours?** TR: 27

## Our Street Party

*Chorus*

*Today was our street party.*
*It was a lot of fun.*
*We all came together.*
*There was something for everyone.*

What did you make?
What did you see?
Tell us all about it, please!

We made decorations. We made costumes.
We saw dance shows. We saw races.
We all came together.
There was something for everyone.
*Chorus*

What did you drink?
What did you eat?
Tell us all about it, please!

We drank milkshakes. We drank fruit juice.
We ate pancakes. We ate pizza.
We all worked together.
And there was something for everyone.
*Chorus*

**2** **Listen and sing.** TR: 28 and 29

**3** **Sing and act.** TR: 30

**VALUE** Be a good neighbour.
*Workbook, Lesson 6*

# Writing An email

LESSON 6

## 1 Read Uma's email. Why was she tired?

**To:** Toby
**From:** Uma
**Subject:** A wedding!

Hi Toby,

How are you? My weekend was fun! Yesterday, it was my aunt's wedding party.

First of all, I went with my mum to help with the preparations. We made big circles of flowers for people to wear around their necks and in their hair. Later, we watched the marriage ceremony. My aunt and uncle drank a special drink. It was milk with banana. After the ceremony, we went home to change our clothes. I wore a blue and gold dress. Then, we went back to the wedding. Everyone danced and sang. At the end, we all threw flower petals on my aunt and uncle! It was beautiful and everyone was very happy.

I went home to bed at 11 o'clock. I was very tired!

See you soon!

Uma

## 2 Read. Then look at Uma's email again and answer the questions.

In an **email describing an event**, we:

- write a subject in the subject line.
- start with a greeting.
- describe what happened.
- say goodbye at the end.

1 What is the subject of her email?
2 How does she say hello and goodbye?
3 What verbs does she use to describe the events?

## 3 Writing skill Time connectors

### a Read and answer the question.

We use these time connectors to explain when things happened.

first of all   then
after (the ceremony)   at the end

Do they go at the beginning or the end of a sentence?

### b Complete Toby's email to Uma with time connectors.

Hi Uma,

That sounds like a great wedding. I had a great Saturday too.

1 ____________, I had a swimming competition, and I came second. 2 ____________, we had lunch in my favourite café. 3 ____________ lunch, my cousins visited us and we went to a summer street party. We watched the school band. They were great! 4 ____________, we said goodbye to our cousins and went home.

See you soon.
Toby

## 4 Write an email to a friend about a celebration you went to.

# LESSON 7 Video

**1** Watch the video. Match the countries (1–3) with the festivals (A–C). ▶ Video 4

1 Japan ☐ 2 the US ☐ 3 Mexico ☐

A

B

C

**2** Watch the video again. Match the children with two things they talk about. ▶ Video 4

1 Yurara C ☐ 2 AJ ☐ ☐ 3 Marlen ☐ ☐

A music and dance
B a festival in August
C fireworks
D taking photos
E sculptures made of sand
F colourful costumes

**3** Answer the questions.

1 Who did Yurara go to the Fireworks festival with?
2 What does she say about the food they had?
3 In which month is the Sandsations festival?
4 What do the artists use to make the sculptures?
5 How long does the Guelaguetza festival last?
6 What does the festival celebrate?

**4** Work in pairs. Discuss the questions.

1 What different festivals are there in your country? Which is your favourite?
2 What festivals and celebrations from other countries do you know about?
3 Which would you like to go to most? Why?

UNIT

# Sport for all 4

Students at a school in Seoul, South Korea

**Look at the photo. Answer the questions.**

1 What sport are they doing?
2 Why do you think they enjoy it?
3 Would you like to do this sport?

LESSON 1 Words

## 1 Listen and repeat. TR: 31

athletics

cycling

diving

golf

gymnastics

ice skating

rowing

sailing

snowboarding

volleyball

## 2 Answer the questions.

1 Which sports need a ball?
2 Which need water, ice or snow?
3 How many can you do?
4 Which would you like to do?

## 3 Listen to the conversation about a Paralympic sport for people who can't see well. Complete the information. TR: 32

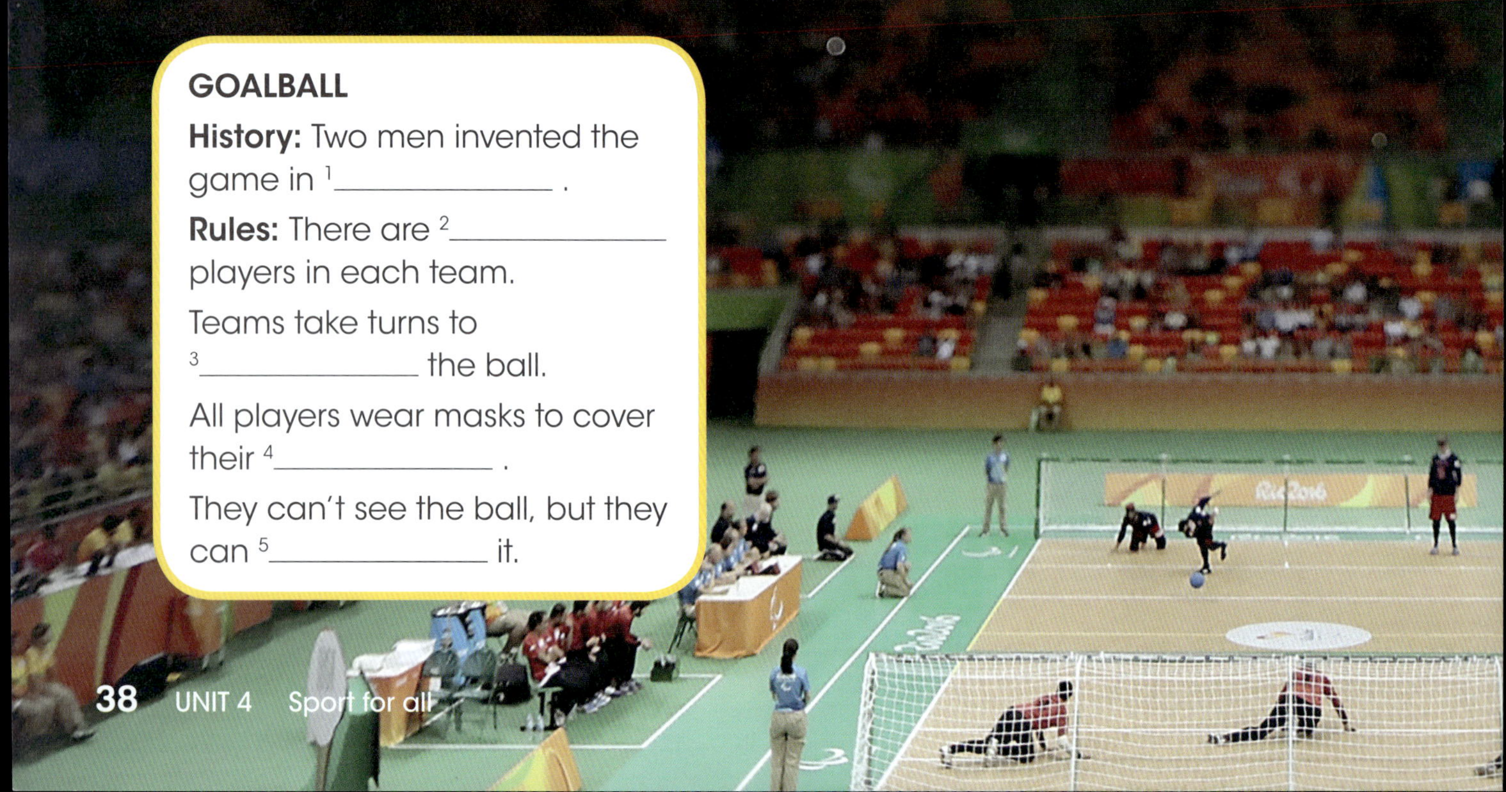

**GOALBALL**

**History:** Two men invented the game in [1]_____________ .

**Rules:** There are [2]_____________ players in each team.

Teams take turns to [3]_____________ the ball.

All players wear masks to cover their [4]_____________ .

They can't see the ball, but they can [5]_____________ it.

Belgium vs Algeria in the 2012 London Paralympic Games

# Grammar

LESSON 2

## 1 Listen and read. TR: 33

***Can* and *could***

**Present**

*They* ***can*** *hear the ball.*

*They* ***can't*** *see the ball.*

**Past**

*They* ***could*** *see, but not very well.*

*They* ***couldn't*** *play any sports.*

## 2 Complete the text with *can, can't, could* or *couldn't*.

Some sports, like golf, volleyball and basketball are difficult for blind people to play. But there are many sports they [1]__________ play. They [2]__________ win medals too. Jen Armbruster is an American goalball player. When she was a teenager, Jen was in the school basketball team. She [3]__________ play really well. But at the age of 14, she began to have eye problems and soon she [4]__________ see at all. Then she [5]__________ play basketball any more. But there was a sport she [6]__________ play: goalball! She joined the Olympic team when she was 16. In 2008, she won a gold medal.

## 3 What could you do at the age of five? Make two sentences.

talk in ... | read | walk | ride a bike | play basketball

*I could read, but I couldn't talk in English.*

## 4 Work in pairs. Ask and answer questions about your sentences from Exercise 3.

Could you play basketball?

No, I couldn't. But I could ride a bike.

LESSON 3
# Reading

**1 Look at the photo. Why is there only one swimmer?**

**2 Listen and read.** TR: 34

### The Olympic dream!

Eric Moussambani was a star at the Olympics in Sydney in 2000. The swimmer from Equatorial Guinea didn't win a medal, but the crowd loved him.

Eric only started swimming in January 2000. He was 21 years old. He practised in a small swimming pool in a hotel. When he saw the Olympic pool in Sydney, he was **surprised**. It was huge! It was 50 metres long. He couldn't see the other end of it! The pool at home was only 12 metres long.

In Eric's race, there were two other swimmers. But they both jumped in the pool too early and the referee stopped the race. When the race started again, Eric was the only swimmer and he was **nervous**. Everyone watched him. He started to swim very quickly, but soon he felt very **tired**. The crowd cheered "Eric! Eric!" This helped him to finish. After the race, Eric was a hero. His time was very slow, but it didn't matter. People thought he was very **brave**.

In 2016, Eric went to the Olympics in Rio de Janeiro, Brazil. He didn't swim for Equatorial Guinea. He was the team's coach!

**3 Answer the questions.**

1 When did Eric start swimming?
2 Where were the Olympic Games in 2000?
3 How long was the pool in the hotel?
4 How did Eric feel before the race?
5 What did the crowd shout?
6 Did Eric finish the race?

**4 Work in pairs. What do these adjectives mean? Then answer the questions.**

brave nervous surprised tired

1 Talk about a person who did something brave.
2 What makes you feel nervous?
3 When was the last time you were surprised?
4 When do you feel tired?

**Eric Moussambani swims alone in the 2000 Olympic Games**

# Grammar

## 1 Listen and read. TR: 35

**Object pronouns**

| | |
|---|---|
| *Can you help **me**?* | *Did you see **us**?* |
| *Can I watch the race with **you**?* | *He waved to **them**.* |
| *Everyone watched **him**.* | |
| *He threw the ball back to **her**.* | |
| *He couldn't see the other end of **it**.* | |

## 2 Complete the text with object pronouns.

**Olympic and Paralympic stories**

- In 1956, a Russian rower, Viktor Ivanov, dropped his silver medal in the lake. A 13-year-old student found [1]______________ in the water and returned it to [2]______________ .
- In 1960, Abebe Bikila won the marathon. His new running shoes didn't fit very well, so he ran without [3]______________ !
- Wilma Rudolph won two gold medals in 1960. She ran in the 100 metres and 200 metres. People called [4]______________ 'the tornado'.
- Derek Redmond fell in a race in 1992. His father helped [5]______________ to finish [6]______________ .

## 3 Complete the questions with object pronouns. Then answer them.

1 What sports do you do? Why do you like doing ______________?

2 Do you do sports alone, or do other people play with ______________?

3 Which sport do you like watching on TV? Do you play ______________ with your friends too?

4 Who is your favourite sportsman? Why do you like ______________?

5 Who is your favourite sportswoman? Why do you like ______________?

LESSON

# 5 Song

**1** **Listen and read. What do you like about doing sport?** TR: 36

## Running for fun

When I was young,
I didn't like sport.
I wasn't good at it.
"It's boring," I thought.

But when I was older,
I went out in the sun.
I started to row.
And I started to run.
… And it was fun!
It didn't matter if I lost or won.
I had fun with my friends.
Yes, I had fun with them!

I didn't like teams.
I didn't like to race.
I wasn't good at it,
Always in last place.

But when I was older,
I went out in the sun.
I started to cycle.
And I started to jump.
… And it was fun!
It didn't matter if I lost or won.
I had fun with my friends.
Yes, I had fun with them!

**2** **Listen and sing.** TR: 37 and 38

**3** **Sing and act.** TR: 39

**VALUE** Have fun doing sport.
*Workbook, Lesson 6*

# Writing A factfile

LESSON 6

**1** **What do you know about these people? Read and find out.**

**2** **Read. Then look at the factfiles again and answer the questions.**

A **factfile** for a person shows you some important information about them. This can include:

- their name and what they do
- personal information, e.g. their birthday and birth place
- facts about things they did in the past.

1 What do these two people do?
2 When were they born?
3 What did they do when they were young?

**3** **Writing skill** Using *when*

**a** **Find *when* in the factfiles. What punctuation do we use after the *when* clause?**

**b** **Match to make sentences about the Australian cyclist, Anna Meares.**

1 When she was young, …
2 When she was 11, …
3 When she was 20, …
4 When she was 28, …

A she won her second Olympic gold medal.
B she started cycling.
C she won her first Olympic gold medal.
D she didn't cycle. She did karate and she played tennis.

**4** **Write a factfile about a famous sportsperson.**

**Name:**
Usain Bolt
**Sport:**
Athletics
**Date of birth:**
21st August, 1986
**Place of birth:**
Jamaica
**Nickname:**
*Lightning Bolt*

* When he was young, he played cricket and football.
* When he was 12, he was the fastest runner in his school at 100 metres.
* When he was 21, he broke the world record for 100 metres.
* Five days before his 22nd birthday, he won his first Olympic gold medal.

**Name:**
Annika Sörenstam
**Sport:**
Golf
**Date of birth:**
9th October, 1970
**Place of birth:**
Sweden
**Nickname:**
*Miss 59*

* When she was young, she liked skiing, tennis and football.
* When she was 12, her parents bought her some golf clubs.
* When she was 16, she played in the Swedish team.
* When she was 24, she won her first big tournament.

LESSON 7
# Video

**1** **Watch the video. Which famous sportspeople do the children talk about?** ▶ Video 5

**2** **Watch the video again. Write B (Bruce Lee), P (Pelé) or W (Wilma Rudolph).** ▶ Video 5

1 _____ could run fast with a football.
2 _____ could run 100 metres in 11 seconds.
3 _____ could do kung fu.
4 _____ couldn't walk when they were young.
5 _____ could score goals with their head.

**3** **Read and write T (true) or F (false).**

1 Bruce Lee was an actor.
2 Bruce Lee died when he was 73.
3 Pelé's real name wasn't *Pelé*.
4 Pelé won the World Cup three times with Brazil.
5 Wilma Rudolph was called 'the tornado' because she was fast.
6 Wilma Rudolph won medals in three Olympic Games.

**4** **Work in pairs. Discuss the questions.**

1 Which person from the video would you like to know more about, and what?
2 Who were some important sportspeople from your country? Why were they famous?
3 Which sport would you like to do well? Why?

**1** Play the game in small groups. Follow the instructions.

**Start**

- What did you do last summer?
- What did you buy on Saturday?
- **Move forward two spaces!**
- What did you eat for lunch yesterday?
- When did you last buy a book?
- What sports could you do when you were six?
- **Move forward three spaces!**
- What time did you have breakfast this morning?
- What did you wear on Sunday?
- When was the last time you celebrated something?
- Where was your first home?
- What did you drink at lunchtime?
- What was the last present you got?
- **Miss a turn!**
- When did you last cycle?
- When did you last swim?
- What did you watch on TV at the weekend?
- What sport did you do this week?
- What did you learn at school today?
- What music did you listen to yesterday?
- **Move forward two spaces!**
- How did you get to school on Monday?
- Who did you talk to first today?
- Where did you go at the weekend?
- What did you eat for dinner yesterday?

**Finish**

**Instructions**

Take turns to throw a coin.

- One side = move forward two spaces
- Other side = move forward one space

You must answer each question with a sentence. You must answer in 15 seconds. If you don't answer correctly, you go back one space. The first player to the FINISH wins!

# The tightrope across Niagara Falls

There was once a famous tightrope walker named Charles Blondin. He lived about 150 years ago. Blondin could do many amazing things on a tightrope: he could stand on one leg; he could sit on a chair; he could stop and make something to eat; he could even walk with his eyes closed.

Blondin came from France, but he did many famous tightrope walks across the Niagara Falls, between Canada and the USA – a distance of 340 metres, and 50 metres above the water. People said that it was impossible and that he could never do it. But Blondin did it, not just once but many times. And each time a crowd waited on the other side of the water to watch him. And each time they cheered loudly when he arrived.

There are many stories about Blondin. People say that one time, he crossed the Falls pushing a wheelbarrow with potatoes in it. The crowd watched. They couldn't believe their eyes. 'Ooh!' and 'Aaah!' they shouted as he walked carefully to the other side. When he arrived, they cheered more loudly than ever.

He put down the wheelbarrow and looked at the crowd.

'So, do you think I can walk back across the Falls with the wheelbarrow?' he asked them.

'Yes, you can!' they all shouted.

'And do you think I can walk back with a man in the wheelbarrow too?' he asked.

'Yes!' they shouted again. 'You are the greatest tightrope walker in the world. You can do anything.'

'OK,' said Blondin. He waited for a moment. 'Then who wants to climb into the wheelbarrow?' he asked. He looked at the people, but they were all very quiet.

**Glossary**

**tightrope** A long rope, high above the ground. Acrobats walk along it.

**wheelbarrow** It has one wheel and two handles. People use it for carrying things.

**cheer** to shout because you like something

**crowd** a big group of people

Jay Cochrane walks on a tightrope across the Niagara Falls.

**1** **Look at the acrobat in the photo. What is he doing? What kind of person do you think he is?**

**2** **Listen and read. Did Blondin walk across Niagara Falls?** TR: 40

**3** **Read again and answer the questions.**

1 What four amazing things could Blondin do on a tightrope?
2 How long was the tightrope across the Niagara Falls?
3 What did Blondin put in the wheelbarrow before he crossed the Niagara Falls?
4 Did the crowd think that Blondin could push a person across the Niagara Falls?
5 Who wanted to climb into the wheelbarrow?

**4** **Complete the sentences. Use one, two or three words in each gap.**

1 No one thought that Blondin ______________ across the Niagara Falls.
2 But Blondin walked across the Falls ______________ than once.
3 ______________________ cheered every time he did it.
4 In one story, ______________ potatoes in Blondin's wheelbarrow.
5 No one in the crowd ______________ to climb into the wheelbarrow.

**5** **Work in pairs. Discuss the questions.**

1 Who thought Blondin could cross the Falls with a person in the wheelbarrow?
2 Why did no one want to climb into the wheelbarrow?
3 Do you think it is a good story? Why? / Why not?

# Review 2: Units 3–4

## 1 Complete.

costume decorations parade party games presents

1 Can you help me to put up the ______________?
2 Are you going to wear a ______________ for this party?
3 There are lots of people playing music in the ______________ this year.
4 Do you give ______________ to people at this festival?
5 What ______________ do children your age play?

## 2 Look and write.

______________ ______________ ______________ ______________ ______________

## 3 Complete the questions with these words. Then answer them in pairs.

who where did was what

1 ______________ did you go yesterday?
2 ______________ did you go with?
3 ______________ did you eat?
4 ______________ the weather good?
5 ______________ you have a good time?

## 4 Make sentences using *can, can't, could* or *couldn't*.

| | ice skate | speak French | run quickly | ride a bike |
|---|---|---|---|---|
| **7 years old** | ✗ | ✗ | ✓ | ✗ |
| **Now** | ✓ | ✓ | ✗ | ✓ |

*When I was seven years old, I couldn't ice skate. Now, I can ice skate.*

## 5 Complete the conversation with object pronouns.

**A:** Felix, there's a competition at the swimming pool this afternoon. I'm going to see [1]______________ with Edu. Why don't you come with [2]______________?

**B:** I'm not sure. My mum is helping [3]______________ with my homework.

**A:** You can ask [4]______________ to help [5]______________ do [6]______________ now. Oh, and my cousins are coming too. I want you to meet [7]______________ .

**B:** OK, great! See [8]______________ there.

# Incredible places

UNIT 5

Antelope Canyon in Arizona, US

**Look at the photo. Answer the questions.**

1 How can you describe this place?
2 What could you do here?
3 Would you like to visit this place? Why? / Why not?
4 What kind of places do you like to visit?

LESSON

# 1 Words

## 1 Listen and repeat. TR: 41

bridge

castle

cave

island

jungle

desert

plant

pyramid

rock

wave

## 2 Complete the text with words from the box.

castle island jungle plants rock waves

Last month, my family and I visited Borneo, an 1____________ in Southeast Asia. On the first day, we went into the 2____________ to see all the animals and 3____________ there! We saw a proboscis monkey sitting on a 4____________ . This monkey had a really big nose! The next day, we went to the beach. My brother and I made a 5____________ in the sand. I surfed the big 6____________ , too!

## 3 Listen to a conversation about Yucatan in Mexico. Circle the correct answer. TR: 42

1 Harry's holiday *started / finished* on Saturday.
2 Harry swam with *sharks / sea turtles*.
3 In the jungles of Yucatan there are more than 1,400 types of *animals / plants*.
4 The pyramids are *near the beach / in the jungle*.
5 The Kukulkan Pyramid is sometimes called *'The Castle' / 'The Square'*.
6 Harry *went / didn't go* inside the Kukulkan Pyramid.

Kukulkan Pyramid in Yucatan, Mexico

# Grammar LESSON 2

## 1 Listen and read. TR: 43

**Comparatives and superlatives**

| | |
|---|---|
| tall | *The pyramid is taller than the trees.* |
| big | *The USA is bigger than Mexico.* |
| large | *The largest building is the Kukulkan Pyramid.* |
| busy | *It's the busiest place in the city.* |

good > better > the best

bad > worse > the worst

far > further > the furthest

## 2 Compare these places. Use comparatives.

- lake / sea
- desert / jungle
- town / village
- castle / school

*A sea is usually larger than a lake.*

## 3 Complete the facts with the superlative form of the adjectives in brackets.

1 In 2018, divers in the Yucatan discovered the __________ (long) underwater cave. It's 347 kilometres long!

2 The __________ (old) paintings in the world are in a cave in northern Spain. They are 40,800 years old!

3 The Atacama Desert in Chile is the __________ (dry) desert in the world.

4 The __________ (hot) ocean in the world is the Indian Ocean.

5 Many people think the __________ (good) waves for surfing are in Australia.

## 4 Write four questions using comparatives and superlatives. Ask and answer with a partner.

- Animals
- Places
- Sports
- Music

What's bigger, an elephant or a rhino?

An elephant is bigger than a rhino.

# LESSON 3 Reading

**1** **Look at the photo. Name three things you see.**

**2** **Listen and read.** TR: 44

### The desert sands!

Dubai is the largest and most **important** city in the United Arab Emirates. Dubai is by the sea, but all the land around it is desert. Many people want to work and live there. The most **popular** place to live is by the beach. It is much cooler there. But there isn't much space to live by the beach any more. In 2001, people started to build the Jumeirah islands on the water. They used rocks and sand to make them. They look like palm trees!

Outside Dubai, there are huge hills of sand called 'dunes'. There are thousands of kilometres of them. There is an **exciting** sport you can do on them: sandboarding! This is the same as snowboarding, but it's on sand instead of snow! It's great fun but you need to be careful too – it is **dangerous** to be in the hot sun for a long time. Drive up to the top of the dunes, then sandboard down. The worst part is that you have to walk back up afterwards!

**3** **Read again. Write T (true) or F (false).**

1 There are other cities in the United Arab Emirates that are bigger than Dubai.
2 In Dubai, people usually want to live near the beach because it is cooler there.
3 People made the Jumeirah islands.
4 There are dunes inside the city of Dubai.
5 There are thousands of kilometres of snow outside Dubai.

**4** **What do the adjectives in bold refer to in the text? Complete the sentences.**

1 Some sports are ______________ if you don't wear a helmet.
2 I hope the film is ______________ . I don't want to see a boring film.
3 It is ______________ that you wear sun cream in the hot sun.
4 Many people visit the shopping centres in Dubai. They are very ______________ places to go.

## 5 Discuss the questions.

1 Would you like to visit Dubai? Why? / Why not?

2 Can you discover more things about Dubai? Tell your partner about them.

One of the Jumeirah islands in Dubai

## 1 Listen and read. TR: 45

**Comparatives and superlatives: long adjectives**

*The homes by the beach are **more popular than** the homes in the city.*

*Dubai is **the most important** city in the United Arab Emirates.*

## 2 Complete the sentences with the comparative or superlative form of the adjectives in brackets.

In 2008, Burj Khalifa became 1 ______________ (tall) building in the world. It's in Dubai. It was one of 2 __________________ (expensive) projects ever. It cost 1.5 billion dollars. It is 3 ______________ (famous) than other buildings in Dubai. I'd love to go there. It has 4 ______________ (high) restaurant in the world too, on the 122nd floor! Some people say that the view from the top is 5 ______________ (exciting) at night than during the day.

## 3 Make sentences about these topics. Use the comparative or superlative form of these adjectives.

- Films
- School subjects
- People
- Free-time activities

dangerous difficult exciting famous important interesting popular

## 4 Work in pairs. Compare your sentences from Exercise 3. Do you agree?

Maths is the most difficult subject.

I don't agree. I think art is the most difficult subject.

LESSON 5 **Song**

**1** **Listen and read. Which place would you like to go to?** TR: 46

### Let's explore!

*Chorus*

*Let's explore! Let's explore!*
*See the world outside our door.*
*There's so much to do and see.*
*So please come along with me!*

Let's go down into a cave!
Are you feeling very brave?
There may be a bat or snake.
But we can swim deep in the lake!
Don't be scared, you're with me.
Just come along and you'll see!
*Chorus*

There's a castle made of stone.
Let's climb up it on our own.
We can see the furthest town,
And the people on the ground.
Climb up, you and me.
Just come along and you'll see!
*Chorus*

**2** **Listen and sing.** TR: 47 and 48

**3** **Sing and act.** TR: 49

VALUE **Explore new places.**
*Workbook, Lesson 6*

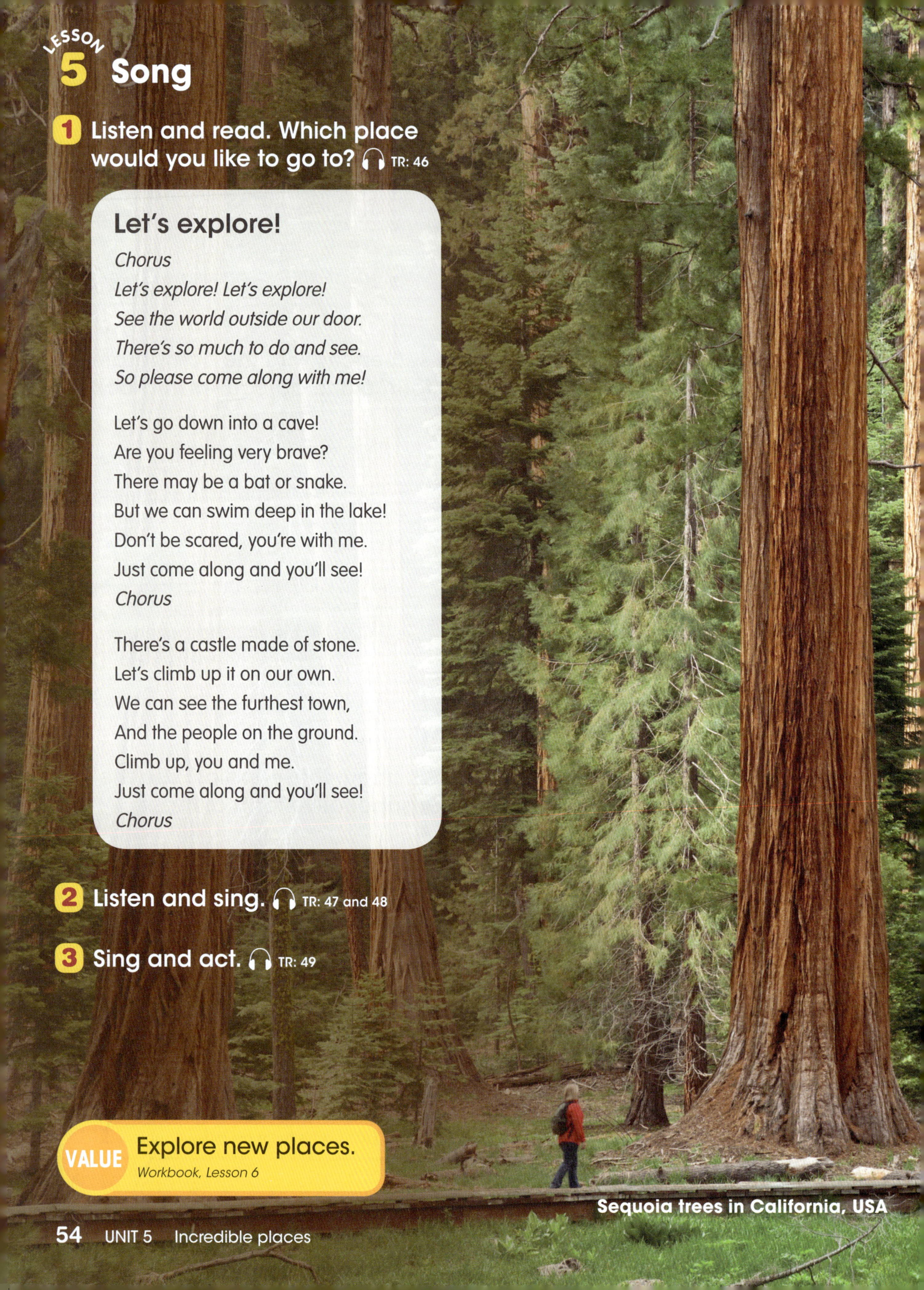

**Sequoia trees in California, USA**

# **Writing** A travel brochure

**1** **Read the travel brochure. Would you like to go there? Why? / Why not?**

**2** **Read. Then look at the travel brochure again and do tasks 1–3.**

A **travel brochure**:
- presents interesting information about a place.
- uses pictures and exciting descriptions.
- gives useful information about visiting a place.

1 Find a sentence that gives information about the place.
2 Find a sentence that makes you want to visit the place.
3 Find a sentence with some useful information.

**3** **Writing skill** Capital letters

**a** **Read the information in the box.**

We use capital letters for:
- the first word of a sentence
- names of people, places and things
- days and months

**b** **Underline the letters that should be capital letters.**

1 she visited finland in october.
2 let's visit jeanne in london on thursday.
3 the george hotel is the best.
4 grandma wants to go to new york.

**4** **Think about a special place. Write a travel brochure.**

## Visit Finland

**Stay warm and enjoy the show!**

People travel to Lapland, Finland from around the world to see the Northern Lights. It's the most amazing natural show. At Kakslauttanen Resort, you can see the Northern Lights from your own igloo! Lie down in your bed and look through the glass roof. You've got the best view of this brilliant show. And you are warmer and more comfortable than the people standing in the snow!

**When to go**
- The best time to see the Northern Lights is between September and March.

**Transport**
- There's a bus to our resort from Ivalo Airport. We also have a bus with a glass roof for large groups!

**What to wear**
- It's very cold in the winter: between 0°C and -40°C. Don't forget your hat, gloves, boots and a warm coat!

**We can't wait to see you!**

LESSON

# 7 Video

**1** **Watch the video. Which country is each place in?** ▶ Video 6

1 Italy ☐   2 Brazil ☐   3 China ☐

A

B

C

**2** **Watch the video again. Complete the sentences with the superlative form of these adjectives.** ▶ Video 6

high (x2)   long (x2)   tall

1 The ______________ mountain in the Dolomites is called Marmolada.
2 The Amazon is one of the ______________ rivers in the world.
3 The ______________ rock in the Zhangjiajie Park is more than 1,000 metres.
4 The Glass Bridge is the ______________ and ______________ bridge in the world.

**3** **Answer the questions.**

1 How high is the Marmolada?
2 What can people do on the lakes?
3 How long is the Amazon river?
4 What do scientists do there?
5 What do the rocks in the Zhangjiajie Park look like?
6 Does the glass skywalk go around a rock, a bridge or a mountain?

**4** **Work in pairs. Discuss the questions.**

1 Which of the places in the video would you like to visit? Why?
2 What's the most popular natural place in your country? Where is it?
3 Why is it popular? What can people do there?

# Cool clothes

UNIT 6

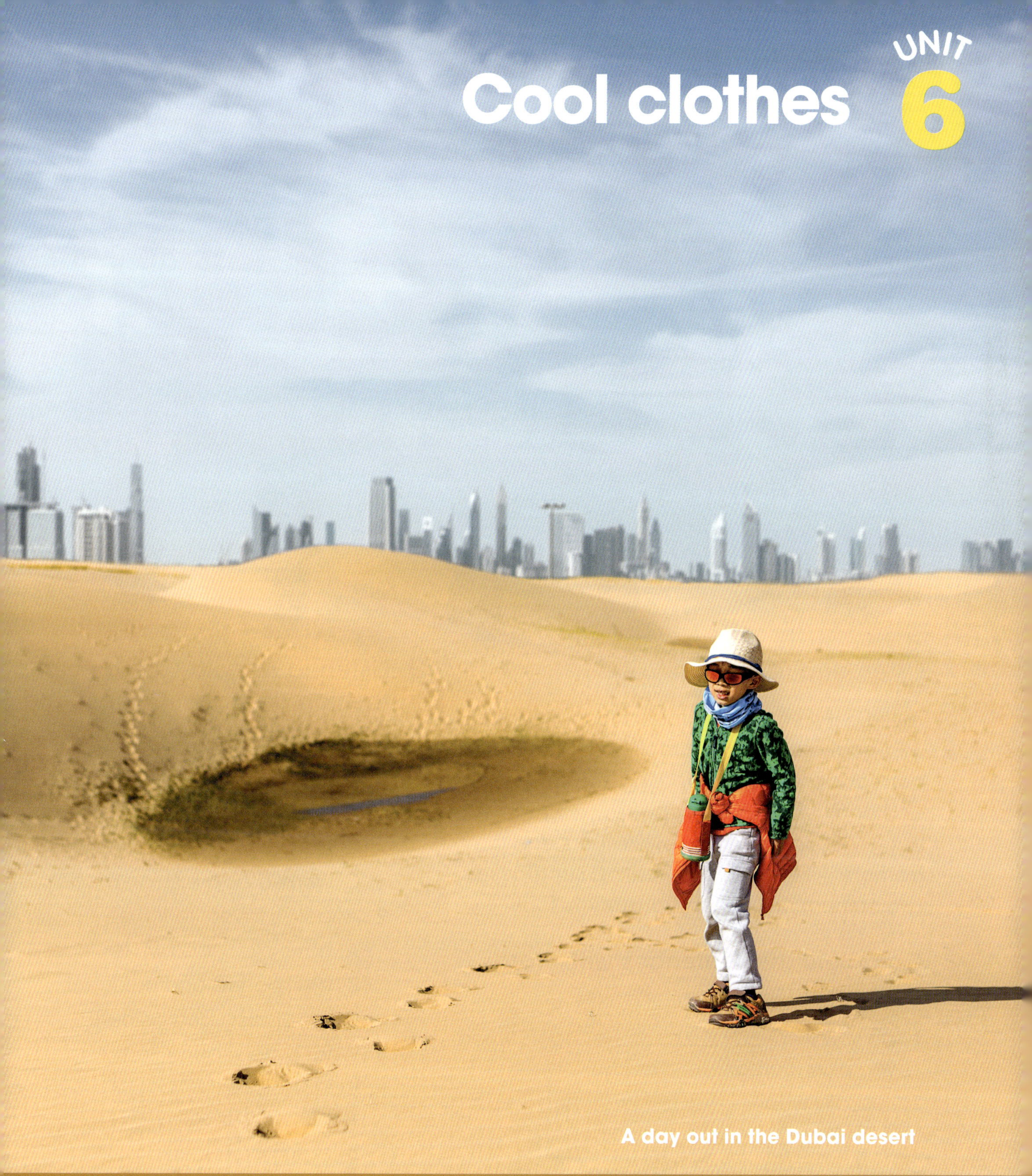
A day out in the Dubai desert

**Look at the photo. Answer the questions.**

1. What is the boy wearing?
2. Do you like his clothes? Why? / Why not?
3. What do you usually wear at the weekend?
4. What's your favourite item of clothing?

LESSON **1**

# Words

## 1 Listen and read. TR: 50

These children are wearing colourful coats with **pockets**. They look really warm and **comfortable**. A girl is wearing **striped leggings** and another is wearing **spotted** leggings. A boy is wearing **plain** yellow trousers and black **trainers**. All the girls are wearing **sunglasses**. Two of them are wearing **bracelets** too!

## 2 Complete the sentences with words from Exercise 1.

1 Do you wear ____________ or boots when you play football?

2 I usually wear ____________ when it's sunny. They protect my eyes.

3 Where are my keys? They're not in my ____________.

4 I can move well in these clothes. They are very ____________.

5 I don't like striped or spotted clothes. I prefer ____________ clothes.

## 3 Listen to Angela Lan, a young fashion designer. Choose the correct answer. TR: 51

1 When she was nine, Angela …
  **A** wrote a book about fashion.
  **B** started to make clothes.
  **C** worked as a fashion model.

2 Angela's favourite trousers …
  **A** have black and white stripes.
  **B** are spotted and colourful.
  **C** are striped and colourful.

3 What's the second item Angela talks about?
  **A** her sunglasses
  **B** a pair of trainers
  **C** a white jacket

4 Angela's favourite coat …
  **A** has big pockets.
  **B** is perfect for warm weather.
  **C** is colourful.

# Grammar

LESSON 2

## 1 Listen and read. TR: 52

**Possessive pronouns**

***Whose*** *striped shirt is this? It's* ***mine****.*

| | |
|---|---|
| *my shoes* | *Those shoes are* ***mine****.* |
| *your hat* | *Is this hat* ***yours****?* |
| *his shirt* | *The red shirt is* ***his****.* |
| *her sunglasses* | *The sunglasses on the table are* ***hers****.* |
| *our towels* | *Those towels are* ***ours****.* |
| *their coats* | *Where are Mina and Jane? Are these coats* ***theirs****?* |

## 2 Complete the sentences with possessive pronouns.

1 You can't use that pen. It's not ____________ .

2 ____________ coat is this? I really like it.

3 **A:** Are these your sunglasses?
**B:** Yes, they're ____________ .

4 Where are Jack and Finn? These drinks are ____________ .

5 No, those trainers aren't ____________ . Her trainers are blue.

## 3 In groups, pass a bag around. Each person puts three objects in the bag. Ask and answer questions about each object.

Whose pencil case is this? Is it yours, Laura?

It isn't mine. Pablo, is it yours?

Yes, it is!

## 4 Design your own clothes. Draw a picture of yourself in these clothes. Describe them to a partner.

Autumn-winter 2016 fashion show in Moscow, Russia

LESSON 3

# Reading

## 1 Listen and read. TR: 53

### Odd Socks Day

We usually wear socks to keep our feet warm. But socks can have a message too!

Who says your socks need to **match**? It was Odd Socks Day on Monday 13th November and we celebrated it at our school last week. We met in the playground at 8.45 before school started. Everyone wore different socks on each foot. It was a lot of fun, but why did we do it?

Well, all week we talked about bullying at school. A bully is a person who **hurts** or **frightens** other people. Older and stronger children sometimes bully the younger, **weaker** children, or children who are different to them. We want to stop bullying at our school. So, on Odd Socks Day, we wear different socks to show everyone that it is good to be different and that all children are important. Everyone needs to feel happy and safe at school.

Let's stop bullying!

## 2 Match the words in bold in the text with their meanings.

1 less strong
2 to look the same as another thing
3 to make someone feel unhappy
4 to make someone feel scared

## 3 Read again. Write T (true) or F (false).

1 Odd Socks Day is next week. ☐
2 School started before 8.45. ☐
3 On Odd Socks Day, students wear socks that match. ☐
4 A bully makes other children feel safe. ☐
5 Children sometimes bully other children who are different to them. ☐

## 4 Discuss the questions.

1 Is Odd Socks Day a good idea? Why? / Why not?

2 What things can you do to help other students feel happy at school?

3 Do you sometimes wear special clothes for a celebration? When?

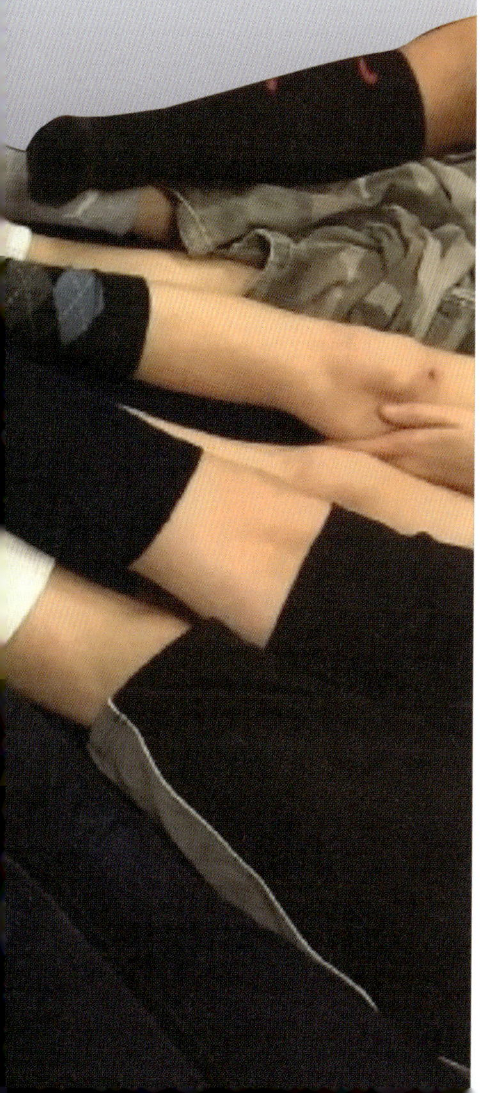

## 1 Listen and read. TR: 54

**Infinitive of purpose**

*We usually wear socks* ***to keep*** *our feet warm.*

*We wear odd socks* ***to show*** *everyone that it is good to be different.*

## 2 Match to make sentences.

| | | | |
|---|---|---|---|
| 1 | We wear hats | A | to protect our eyes. |
| 2 | We wear sunglasses | B | to keep our hands warm. |
| 3 | We use umbrellas | C | to show that we like a team. |
| 4 | We wear football shirts | D | to keep our heads warm. |
| 5 | We wear gloves | E | to protect us from the rain. |

## 3 What do you use each object for? Discuss.

1 

2 

3 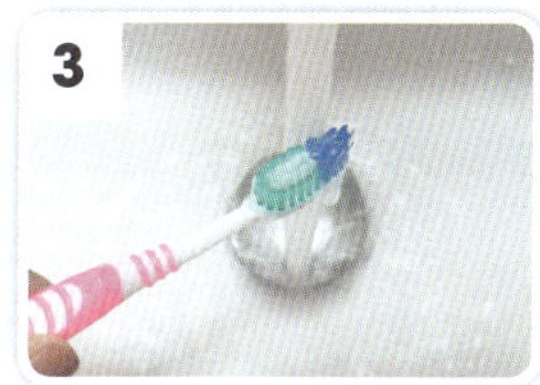

4 

5 

6 

*I use a smartphone to call my parents.*

## 4 Work in pairs. You're on a desert island. Choose four of these objects and explain how you can use them.

blanket bottle helmet jacket map
MP3 player smartphone soap toothbrush towel

I want to bring a bottle. I can use it to carry water.

LESSON 5

# Song

**1 Listen and read. What's your favourite thing in the whole world?** TR: 55

## Now it's mine!

Look at the scarf I'm wearing today.
My great-grandad wore it to keep him warm.
Then he gave it to my grandad.
He gave it to my mum.
And now it's mine!

*Chorus*
*It's my favourite thing in the whole world.*
*It's my favourite thing in the whole world.*
*I must look after it well.*
*Who's going to have it next?*

Look at the umbrella I'm using today.
My great-grandma used it to keep her dry.
Then she gave it to my uncle.
He gave it to my dad.
And now it's mine!
*Chorus*

Look at the bracelet I'm wearing today.
My grandma wore it to give her luck.
Then she gave it to my aunt.
She gave it to my mum.
And now it's mine!
*Chorus*

**2 Listen and sing.** TR: 56 and 57

**3 Sing and act.** TR: 58

**VALUE** Look after your things.
*Workbook, Lesson 6*

# **Writing** An invitation

## 1 Read the invitation. Would you like to go to this party?

**Dear** Freya
**Please come to my party!** It's a pizza, film and sleepover party!
**Date:** 20th and 21st February
**Time:** 5.30pm on Saturday to 11am on Sunday
**Place:** 63 Lakeside Road (It's next to the library.)
**Remember to bring:** pyjamas, a toothbrush (and your favourite teddy if you want!)
On Friday evening, we're going to eat pizza and watch a film. In the morning, we're going to play tennis, so bring shorts and trainers with you too! You don't need a racket. You can use one of mine.
Text Helen (my mum) to say if you can come. Her number is 07700 900368.
I hope you can come!
Sarah

## 2 Read. Then look at the invitation again and answer the questions.

An **invitation** asks you to come to a party or a celebration. It includes:

- who the invitation is for and who it is from
- what kind of party it is
- the date and time
- the place
- any other important information.

1 When is the party?
2 Where is the party?
3 Who is the invitation for?
4 Who is the invitation from?

## 3 Writing skill Times, dates, addresses

**a Read.**

Time: use *am* (morning) or *pm* (afternoon or evening).
Date: write *st, nd* or *th* after the numbers.
Address: write the number of the house first and then the name of the street or road.

**b Underline and correct the mistakes on this invitation.**

**Please come to my party!**
It's a costume party!
**Date:** *10st March*
**Time:** *11.30pm before lunch*
**Place:** *Ship Street, 34*

## 4 Think about a party you'd like to have. Write an invitation for a friend.

## LESSON 7 Video

**1** **Watch the video. Which country has these special clothes?** Video 7

1 Morocco ☐ 2 Saudi Arabia ☐ 3 Vietnam ☐

A

B

C

**2** **Watch the video again. Tick (✓) the clothes that you hear.** Video 7

| | | | |
|---|---|---|---|
| pockets ☐ | hat ☐ | dresses ☐ | trousers ☐ |
| sunglasses ☐ | shoes ☐ | coat ☐ | scarves ☐ |

**3** **Circle the correct answer.**

1 A 'gandoura' *has / hasn't* got pockets.
2 A 'shesh' is usually *colourful / black*.
3 People wear rice hats to *protect them from the sun and rain / keep their heads warm*.
4 The traditional 'ao dai' dress is *colourful / white*.
5 A 'thobe' has *long / short* sleeves.
6 'Shemaghs' are *always / sometimes* red and white.

**4** **Work in pairs. Discuss the questions.**

1 What special clothes do people wear in your country?
2 What do these clothes look like? When do people wear them?
3 Do you like to wear special clothes? Why? / Why not?

| | |
|---|---|
| Can I help you? | Yes, please. |
| **I'm looking for** a striped shirt. | |
| **How much is** this jacket? | **It's** 120 euros. |
| **What size are you?** | Small./Medium./Large. |
| **Here's a** lovely dress. | **I'll take** it! |

## 1 Listen and complete. TR: 59

**Customer:** Good afternoon!
**Shop assistant:** Hello. Can I help you?
**Customer:** Yes, please. I'm looking for a new [1]__________ .
**Shop assistant:** What colour do you want?
**Customer:** [2]__________ , please.
**Shop assistant:** OK. Here's a nice [3]__________ .
**Customer:** Ooh, I like it. It's very nice.
**Shop assistant:** Great. What size are you?
**Customer:** [4]__________ .
**Shop assistant:** Perfect! Here you are.
**Customer:** I'll take it! Oh, but wait. How much is it?
**Shop assistant:** It's [5]__________ euros.
**Customer:** Oh, that's very expensive!

## 2 Listen, check and repeat. TR: 60

## 3 Complete the mini dialogues.

1 **Shop assistant:** ____________________ .
**Customer:** Yes, please. I'm looking for a new hat.

2 **Customer:** ____________________ .
**Shop assistant:** It's 50 euros.

3 **Customer:** I'm looking for brown shoes.
**Shop assistant:** ____________________ .
**Customer:** I'm size 39.

## 4 Role-play a dialogue between a shop assistant and a customer.

# Hang Son Doong

This video is about a cave in Vietnam, called Hang Son Doong. It's the largest cave in the world. There's a fast river inside the cave too. The cave is more than five kilometres long. In two places, the top of the cave fell in many years ago. So, the sun shines in and trees and plants grow there. Some of the largest stalagmites in the world are here too. Stalagmites are long rocks that point up from the floor of the cave. Some of these are about 70 metres tall.

**1 Read about the biggest cave in the world. Answer the questions.**

1 How long is the Hang Son Doong cave?
2 Why are there many plants and trees growing in the cave?

**2 Watch the video. Circle the correct answer.** ▶ Video 8

1 Ho Khanh could see *water* / *clouds* coming from the cave.
2 Hang Son Doong means *Mountain River Cave* / *Long Beautiful Cave*.
3 The cave is *18* / *3* million years old.
4 Some parts of the cave are 200 *metres* / *kilometres* tall.
5 It takes about *three* / *five* days to walk from the road to the entrance of the cave.

**3 PROJECT Work in pairs. Make a cave.**

Make a model of a cave with stalagmites and stalactites. Use black and grey paper, scissors and glue.

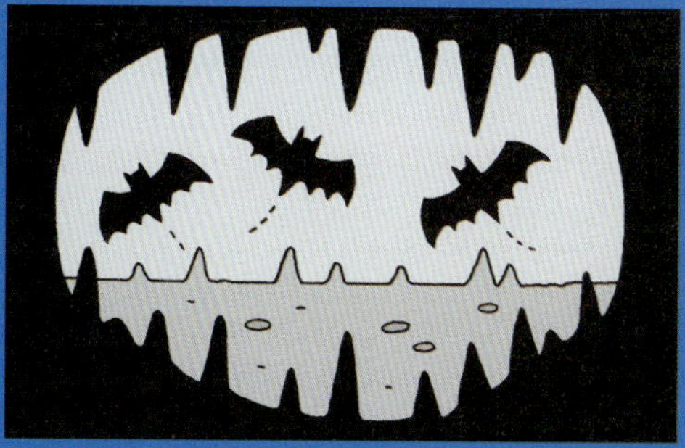

**4 Find out about an interesting cave. Tell the class about it.**

This cave in Spain is very old. It has paintings on the wall.

# Review 3: Units 5–6

## 1 Read, choose and write.

bridge island plain pockets sunglasses waves

1 without a design (e.g. not spotted or striped) __________
2 You walk on this to go across a river. __________
3 This is land that has water all around it. __________
4 The lines of water that move on top of the sea. __________
5 These are on clothes and you can keep things inside them. __________
6 You wear these to protect your eyes from the sun. __________

## 2 Where does each person want to go? Listen and write a letter in each box. TR: 61

1 Eva ☐ 2 Carlos ☐ 3 Sofia ☐ 4 Harry ☐

A

B

C

D

E

F

## 3 Write answers with a possessive pronoun.

1 Whose striped socks are these? *They're mine.* (I)
2 Whose plain red shirt is this? __________ (she)
3 Whose shoes are these? __________ (they)
4 Whose striped shirt is this? __________ (he)
5 Whose spotted socks are those? __________ (we)

## 4 Write sentences about these topics using these adjectives.

- Sports
- Food
- Books
- Films

best worst more interesting more popular most difficult

# Look 4A COMBO SPLIT WORKBOOK

# Look and remember

LESSON 1

**1** **These four men work in the National Park. Who is Mr Place? Read the description and tick (✓) the box.**

A ☐ B ☐ C ☐ D ☐

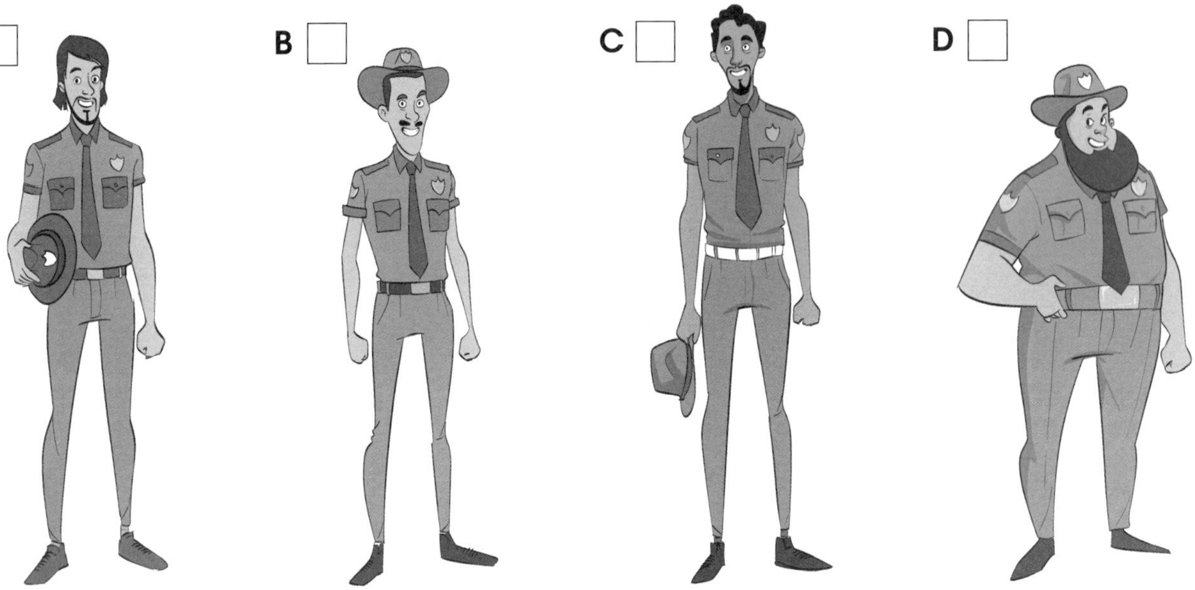

Mr Place has got dark hair. It's curly and it isn't very long. He's short, strong and has got a round face. His sister says he needs to get thinner! He's got a dark beard, but he hasn't got a moustache.

**2** **Write a description of one of the other men in Exercise 1.**

________________________________________

________________________________________

________________________________________

**3** **Complete the sentences about you. Use *always, usually, sometimes* or *never.***

1 I ______________ go shopping at the weekend.
2 I ______________ walk to school.
3 I ______________ make my bed before I go to school.
4 I ______________ read comic books with my friends.
5 I ______________ play hide-and-seek after school.
6 I ______________ make new friends on holiday.

## 4 Listen and tick (✓) the correct answer. TR: 1

1 What does the boy like doing at the weekend?

A ☐

B ☐

C ☐

2 Where does the girl like going on holiday?

A ☐

B ☐

C ☐

3 What does the girl like eating when she goes to the café?

A ☐

B ☐

C ☐

## 5 Answer the questions.

1 Are you and your family going to a theme park this weekend?
*No, we're not. We're going to the forest.*

2 Are you going to go canoeing in the evening?
______________________________

3 Is your mum going to visit a museum tomorrow?
______________________________

4 Is your dad going to sleep in a tent this weekend?
______________________________

5 Are you and your family going to eat outside this evening?
______________________________

6 Are you going to climb a tree tomorrow?
______________________________

7 Are you and your family going to have a picnic this weekend?
______________________________

LESSON 2

## 1 Listen to a person talking about African penguins. Circle the correct answer. TR: 2

1 African penguins live on the *beach* / *ice*.
2 Part of their face is pink above their *eyes* / *mouth*.
3 They put *coconuts* / *shells* next to their eggs to protect them from birds.
4 Sharks and sometimes *cats* / *dogs* try to catch and eat African penguins.
5 African penguins sometimes sound like *chickens* / *donkeys*.

## 2 Read about emperor penguins. Correct the sentences.

Emperor penguins are the biggest bird in the penguin family. They can be more than one metre tall and they usually live for fifteen years. Penguins can't fly, but they are very good at swimming. They can stay underwater for about twenty minutes. They have to be careful when they swim because whales try to catch them. They live in the Antarctic and eat fish. When penguins have an egg, the male penguin puts it on its feet and the female penguin goes to get food.

1 Emperor penguins are smaller than other penguins.

_______________________________________________

2 They are very bad swimmers.

_______________________________________________

3 They can't swim underwater for more than 10 minutes.

_______________________________________________

4 They live in the Arctic.

_______________________________________________

5 The male penguin keeps the egg in its mouth.

_______________________________________________

## 3 Match to make questions.

| | | |
|---|---|---|
| 1 | How many | doing right now? |
| 2 | Where do | your mum or your dad? |
| 3 | Where are | like doing at the weekend? |
| 4 | Who is older – | brothers and sisters have you got? |
| 5 | What does your family | your grandparents live? |
| 6 | What are you | your parents from? |

## 4 Write your answers to the questions in Exercise 3.

1 ____________________
2 ____________________
3 ____________________
4 ____________________
5 ____________________
6 ____________________

UNIT 1

# All kinds of jobs

LESSON 1

## Words

### 1 Look. Write the letters in order.

1 

oraotphgreph

*photographer*

2 

optil

_______________

3 

rwtiea

_______________

4 

rusen

_______________

5 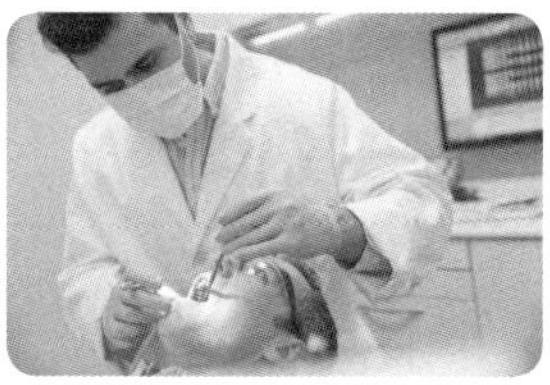

nestdit

_______________

6 

nlocw

_______________

### 2 Listen and complete. TR: 3

1 Laura's aunt is a(n) _______________ .

2 Her mum is a(n) _______________ .

3 Her dad is a(n) _______________ .

4 Her uncle is a(n) _______________ .

5 Laura wants to be a(n) _______________ .

### 3 Read the clues and write the job.

1 Jin can't fly planes. He hasn't got a camera. He likes keeping people safe.

What's Jin's job? _______________

2 Aju helps people but doesn't take food to them. She never looks in people's mouths. She's sometimes very hot at work.

What's Aju's job? _______________

### 4 Choose a job and write four clues for it. Can your partner guess your job?

I _______________________________ .

I _______________________________ .

I _______________________________ .

I _______________________________ .

What's my job?

# Grammar

*See page 122.*

## 1 Complete the sentences with the verbs in brackets. Use the present simple or the present continuous.

1 Ali usually *carries* (carry) heavy trays with plates and glasses. He ______________ (not carry) any today because he's got a sore shoulder.

2 Carlos ______________ (not drive) a police car today. He only ______________ (drive) one on Thursdays and Fridays.

3 Every day, Bruno ______________ (take) photos. Right now, he ______________ (take) a photo of a big waterfall.

4 Natalia ______________ (fly) a plane to France now, and later she's going to fly it to Russia. She ______________ (fly) to eight different countries every week.

5 Osman and Sena ______________ (fight) house fires every week, but right now they ______________ (not fight) a house fire. They ______________ (fight) a forest fire.

6 Amaya ______________ (give) medicine to a young girl right now. She ______________ (give) medicine to a lot of people in hospital every day.

## 2 Match the sentences in Exercise 1 with the photos. Write the jobs.

A ☐ ______________

B ☐ ______________

C ☐ ______________

D ☐ ______________

E ☐ ______________

F ☐ ______________

## 3 Write questions about the person in the photo. Use some of these words and the correct form of the verbs in brackets.

every day   how   right now   today   what   where

1 ______________________________ ? (do)

2 ______________________________ ? (make)

3 ______________________________ ? (feel)

## 4 Answer the questions in Exercise 3.

1 ______________________________

2 ______________________________

3 ______________________________

# LESSON 3 Reading

## 1 Complete.

animated designer director models

1 Hans Weise likes being a film ______________ because he's in charge.
2 Fernando is a good ______________ because he is very good at art.
3 Hans and Fernando worked together on an ______________ film about the Vikings.
4 In the Vikings animation, they used small ______________ of Viking ships.

## 2 Read and complete. Use the correct form of six of these words.

actor big camera idea make move photo waiter

### Walking With Giants

Hans Weise is a film director. He [1]______________ many different kinds of films. He likes making animated films. There aren't usually any [2]______________ in these films. Hans uses models instead. He works with a designer, Fernando Baptista, to make models of the people, places and objects. Fernando paints the models and then Hans takes photos of them. After he takes a photo, he [3]______________ the models. Then he takes another photo. At the end, he puts all the [4]______________ together to make a film. This is called 'stop-motion animation'.

*Walking With Giants* is about the statues on Easter Island, a small island in the middle of the Pacific Ocean. The statues are very [5]______________ and heavy. How did they get there? No one knows for sure, but there are different [6]______________ . Hans and Fernando make animations with models to show these ideas. One idea is that people moved the statues there a long time ago. Hans and Fernando use toy dolls as models of the people. *Walking With Giants* is about four minutes long, but it was four weeks' work!

## 3 Read again. Write T (true) or F (false).

1 Hans Weise only makes animated films. _____
2 Fernando Baptista is an actor in one of Hans Weise's films. _____
3 Hans makes his animations with a lot of photos of models. _____
4 *Walking With Giants* is an animated film about some big statues. _____
5 Hans and Fernando moved the statues to an island. _____

# Grammar

See page 122.

## 1 Listen and match. TR: 4

How often …

1 are there filmmaking classes at camp in the morning? — C

2 do the children visit famous places?

3 do they play tennis at camp?

4 do they do activities in the evening?

5 does Anna make films at home?

6 does Anna learn to make films at school?

A rarely

B often

C usually

D never

E sometimes

F always

## 2 Write sentences with the information from Exercise 1.

1 *There are usually filmmaking classes at camp in the morning.*

2 ______

3 ______

4 ______

5 ______

6 ______

## 3 What do you do on holiday? Complete the sentences. Use adverbs of frequency and these verbs.

be do fly go have visit

1 I ______ homework.

2 I ______ museums.

3 My family ______ in a plane.

4 I ______ to a beach.

5 I ______ happy.

6 My friends and I ______ fun together.

LESSON 5

# Writing An interview

## 1 Tick (✓) the questions that you can use to interview someone about their job.

- [ ] **1** What's your favourite free-time activity?
- [ ] **2** What time do you usually finish work?
- [ ] **3** What's your job?
- [ ] **4** Where do you work?
- [ ] **5** What time is it?
- [ ] **6** What do you do at work every day?

## 2 Complete the interview with questions from Exercise 1.

**INTERVIEW: JAY DICKMAN**

1 ____________________

I'm a photographer.

2 ____________________

All around the world. At the moment, I'm working in the Galápagos Islands, in Ecuador.

3 ____________________

Every day is different. I often teach other people and that's great because I love talking about photography. I sometimes write books about it too. But I usually take photos – of people, of places, of animals.

4 ____________________

When it's dark. The time just before dark is my favourite time of day for taking photos.

## 3 Choose a cool job. You are going to interview a person who does this job. Write four questions using some of these words.

favourite how right now what when where why

1 ____________________?

2 ____________________?

3 ____________________?

4 ____________________?

## 4 Find out the answers to your questions in Exercise 3, or think of your own answers. Then write your interview.

**1** ____________________

**2** ____________________

**3** ____________________

**4** ____________________

**VALUE** Be curious.

## 1 Read the table. Write the job.

| Job: ______________________ | | |
|---|---|---|
| **What I know …** | **What I want to know …** | **What I learnt …** |
| *They want to help people.* | *How do people learn the job?* | 1 ____________ |
| *They know a lot about teeth.* | *Do they often work at the weekend?* | 2 ____________ |
| *A lot of people think they're scary.* | *Is it a fun job?* | 3 ____________ |
| | *Do they have healthy teeth?* | 4 ____________ |

## 2 Match the notes (A–D) with the gaps in the table (1–4) in Exercise 1.

*A. They usually have healthy teeth because they know what is good and bad for teeth.*
*B. They go to university for many years.*
*C. They rarely work on Saturdays or Sundays.*
*D. A lot of people enjoy it, but not everyone!*

## 3 Choose a job and complete the first two columns. Then find out information and complete the last column.

| Job: ______________________ | | |
|---|---|---|
| **What I know …** | **What I want to know …** | **What I learnt …** |
| ____________ | ____________ | ____________ |
| ____________ | ____________ | ____________ |
| ____________ | ____________ | ____________ |
| ____________ | ____________ | ____________ |

## 4 How can you find out things that you don't know? Tick (✓) the best ideas and write one more.

1 I can ask my parents. ☐
2 I can ask my pets. ☐
3 I can read information on the Internet. ☐
4 I can read books from the library. ☐
5 I can look under my bed. ☐
6 I can go to museums. ☐
7 I can ______________ . ☐

# UNIT 2 Move to the music!

## LESSON 1 Words

**1 Look and complete.**

1 
2 
3 
4 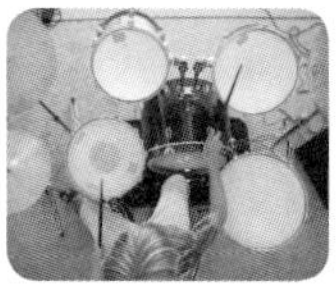
5 
6 
7 
8 
9 

**What's the mystery word?** ________________ music

**2 Listen to two friends talking about a concert. Write T (true) or F (false).** TR: 5

1 The girl wants to go to a concert on Saturday. _____
2 Z Machines is a music group from China. _____
3 Z Machines play classical music. _____
4 A robot named Cosmo plays the keyboard. _____
5 A robot named Ashura plays the drums. _____
6 There aren't any singers or dancers at the concert. _____

**3 Design your own music robot. Draw and write about it.**

My robot's name is ________________ .
________________ can ________________
________________ .
________________ usually plays
________________ music.

## Grammar

See page 123.

**1 Complete the text with the verbs in brackets. Use the past simple.**

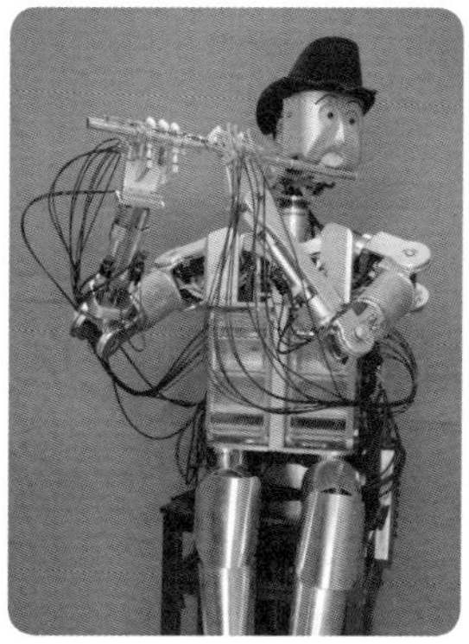

Yesterday, I 1______________ (watch) some music videos. In the first video, there 2______________ (be) a robot with a violin, but I 3______________ (not like) the music very much. Then a robot 4______________ (play) some very fast music on the flute. I 5______________ (love) it! In the last video, the robot 6______________ (not play) an instrument. It 7______________ (move) its arms and an orchestra 8______________ (play) the music. All three robots 9______________ (be) amazing!

**2 Listen and circle the correct answer.** TR: 6

1. The girl *played* / *didn't play* a computer game on Saturday.
2. The robots in the video *danced* / *didn't dance* to classical music.
3. The girl thinks the dancing *was* / *wasn't* amazing.
4. The robots *were* / *weren't* very big.
5. The robots *moved* / *didn't move* like real people.
6. The robots *kicked* / *didn't kick* their legs.

**3 Complete the questions in the past simple. Listen again and write the answers.** TR: 7

1. ______________________ the video at a basketball game? (the girl, watch)
   ______________________
2. ______________________ in the US? (the robots, be)
   ______________________
3. ______________________ the music? (the girl, like)
   ______________________
4. ______________________ in the same way? (all the robots, dance)
   ______________________
5. ______________________ good? (the video, be)
   ______________________

LESSON 3

# Reading

## 1 Complete the sentences with these verbs.

banged carried climbed shouted

There was a programme about some incredible dancers from India. In Odisha, the dancers [1]______________ 'Haido!' when the singer was quiet. In Rajasthan, some dancers [2]______________ eight bowls on their heads! The musicians [3]______________ their drums for the dance. They were very loud. In Karnataka, the dancers [4]______________ onto drums!

## 2 Read. Put the sentences in the correct place. Write the letter on the line.

**A** Then they banged their drums quickly.
**B** You can watch these dancers playing their drums in one of our programmes.
**C** We wanted to learn more about dance and music in India, and we wanted to make a film.
**D** They wear colourful costumes and many of them play the drums.

**Indian music and dance**

My name is Soumik Datta. My brother, Souvid, is a photographer. We live in England, but we were born in India. [1]_____ So, in 2015, we visited India and saw more than 100 different musicians.

One group of musicians from Karnataka is famous for its dance called 'the Kunitha'. [2]_____ They sing and jump too. All the men are farmers, but they love dancing.

We filmed their show. It was incredible! The dancers carried big drums and they banged them loudly. They all shouted and they kicked their feet. Then they played their drums quietly and some of the dancers climbed onto the drums to make a tower. [3]_____ It was very exciting.

[4]_____ We hope you enjoy it!

## 3 Read again. Answer the questions.

1 Where do Soumik and Souvid Datta live? ______________________
2 Which country did they visit in 2015? ______________________
3 Do the farmers like doing the Kunitha dance? ______________________
4 What instrument did the Karnataka musicians play? ______________________
5 Did Soumik enjoy the Kunitha dance? ______________________

# Grammar

See page 123.

## 1 Complete the text with the adverbs of the words in brackets.

One of my favourite Indian dances is the Bhavai dance. At the beginning, the musicians play their music [1]__________ (quiet) and a dancer puts a bowl on her head. Then another person helps the dancer. This person puts a second bowl [2]__________ (careful) on top of the first bowl, so there are two bowls on the dancer's head. Then the helper puts on a third bowl, a fourth, a fifth, and sometimes more. When the dancer has a lot of bowls on her head, the musicians play [3]__________ (loud). The dancer walks [4]__________ (slow) and moves her arms [5]__________ (quick). It's amazing! Some Bhavai dancers can dance [6]__________ (good) with ten bowls on their heads! A lot of people come to this part of India to watch this amazing dance.

## 2 Look and complete the sentences with adverbs.

**1** It's moving __________ .

**2** She's talking __________ .

**3** She's driving __________ .

**4** She's walking __________ .

**5** He's playing the drums __________ .

**6** He can't walk very __________ .

## 3 Complete the sentences about you. Use the adverbs of these words.

bad careful good loud quick quiet slow

**1** I usually run __________ in PE lessons.
**2** I don't like singing __________ .
**3** I usually talk __________ in class.
**4** I can ride a bike __________ .
**5** I usually eat my dinner __________ .

LESSON 5

# Writing A review

## 1 Complete the sentences. Use *because* and the past simple.

1 

The children clapped loudly
*because they loved* the show.

2 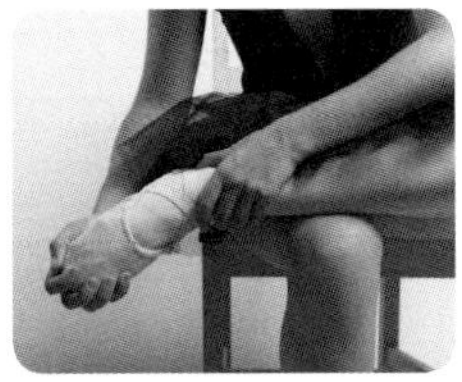

I stopped dancing
______________________ sore.

3 

We laughed ______________________
very badly.

4 

Jon's mother painted his nose red
______________________ in the show.

## 2 Think about a film you saw. Circle and complete.

1 The film was called ______________________ .
2 I saw it last *week* / *month* / *year*.
3 It was about ______________________ .
4 I *liked* / *didn't like* the actors because ______________________ .
5 I *liked* / *didn't like* the story because ______________________ .
6 I *liked* / *didn't like* the ending because ______________________ .
7 There *was some* / *wasn't any* singing.
8 There *was some* / *wasn't any* dancing.

## 3 Write a review of the film you chose in Exercise 2.

Last ______________, I saw a film called ______________________ .
It was about ______________________ .

I really liked the ______________________
______________________
______________________ .

At the end, I ______________________ because ______________________
______________________
______________________ .

VALUE Be yourself.

## 1 Read and circle the letter. What's the best answer for you?

1 Which types of dancing do you like?

A 

B 

C 

D 

2 Which is your favourite place for dancing?

**A** My bedroom, because people can't see me there.
**B** Performances, because everyone is watching me.
**C** Parties, because my friends and I can do the same dance together.
**D** Dance class, because we learn new ways to dance.

3 What do you do when a friend does an unusual free-time activity?

**A** I laugh because unusual activities aren't very cool.
**B** I ask about it.
**C** I want to do the activity too.
**D** I want to try it too, but I worry that people will laugh at me.

4 Do you and your friends like the same things?

**A** No. We're different people and we like different things.
**B** Sometimes, but we like different things too.
**C** Usually. Maybe that's why we're friends.
**D** Yes. We can't be friends if we like different things.

## 2 Circle the best answer.

1 *Dance* / *Don't dance* however you want.
2 *Be* / *Don't be* kind when your friends do their own thing.
3 *Laugh* / *Don't laugh* at people because they're different to you.
4 *Always* / *Don't always* do the same things as your friends.

## 3 Play a song and dance however you want. When you finish, complete the sentences about you.

I danced ______________ . It was ______________ to dance like this.
I was ______________ while I was dancing.

# Function 1: Giving directions

See page 128.

## 1 Look and write.

Go straight on. It's on the left. It's on the right.
Turn left. Turn right. Where is ...?

______

______

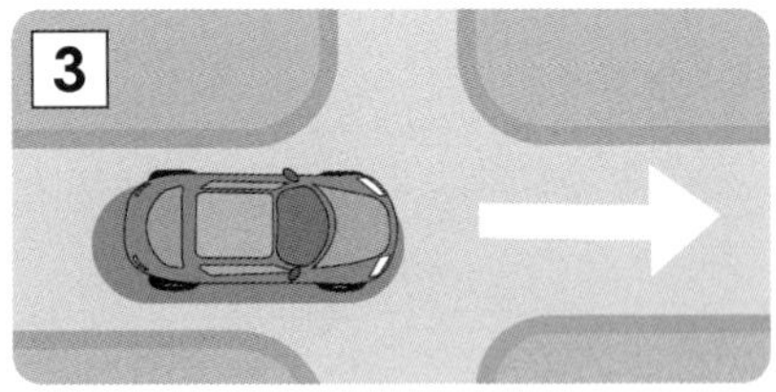


______

______

______

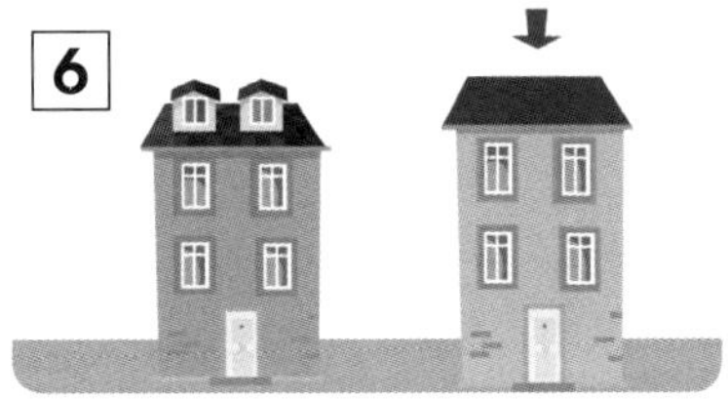


______

## 2 Listen and circle the correct answer. TR: 8

**A:** Can you help me, please? I'm lost. Where's the [1] *cinema / shopping centre*?
**B:** Go straight on and turn [2] *left / right* at the bus stop.
**A:** OK, and then?
**B:** Go straight on and it's on the [3] *left / right*. It's opposite the [4] *restaurant / supermarket*.
**A:** Is it next to a [5] *car park / factory*?
**B:** No, it's next to a [6] *hospital / café*.
**A:** That's great. Thanks!

## 3 Listen again and look at the map. Write the places and draw a line to show the route. TR: 9

1 ______
2 ______
3 ______
4 ______

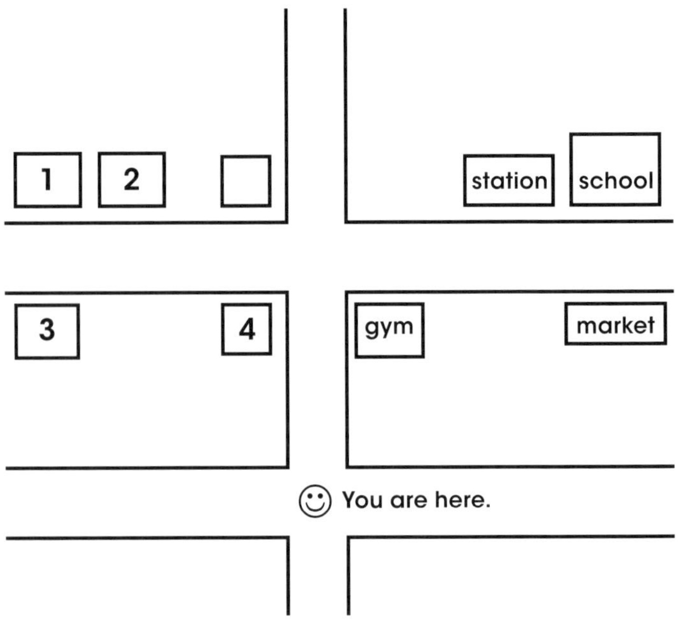


## 4 Look at the map again. Start at the ☺ and write directions to get to the school.

# School trip 1: Redwood forests

**1** **Tick (✓) the things you saw in the video. Then draw three more things you saw.**

**2** **Answer the questions about Nick Nichols.**

1 What's Nick's job?

2 Where does Nick work?

3 Why does he wear special clothes?

4 Why does he take photos of nature?

**3** **Imagine you're a wildlife photographer. What animal do you want to photograph? Draw a picture of the animal and write about it.**

1 Where does the animal live?

2 When is the best time and place to take the photo?

3 Do you need any special clothes?

4 What is the animal doing in your picture?

5 Do you have to wait a long time to take the photo? Why?

# Review 1: Units 1–2

**1** **Find nine words about music.**

| | | | | | | | | |
|---|---|---|---|---|---|---|---|---|
| C | D | O | Y | O | P | U | L | I |
| E | K | E | Y | B | O | A | R | D |
| L | V | K | E | C | P | L | S | A |
| L | I | D | R | U | M | A | I | N |
| O | O | S | S | I | U | C | N | C |
| F | L | U | T | E | S | A | G | E |
| L | I | M | U | S | I | I | E | R |
| C | N | C | O | N | C | E | R | T |

**Write the extra letters to make the question. Then write your answer.**

______________________________?

____________________

**2** **Write sentences about the pictures using these phrases.**

clean people's teeth ~~fly planes~~ have a picnic help ill people ~~listen to music~~ play computer games read a comic take photos

1  *The pilot flies planes, but today she's listening to music at home.* 

2 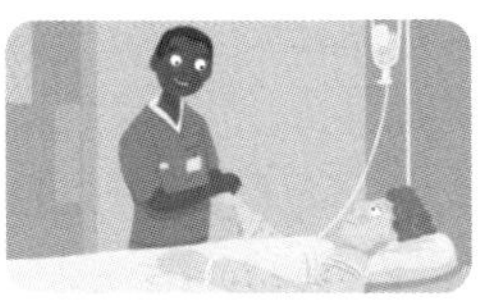 ______________________________ ______________________________ 

3  ______________________________ ______________________________ 

4 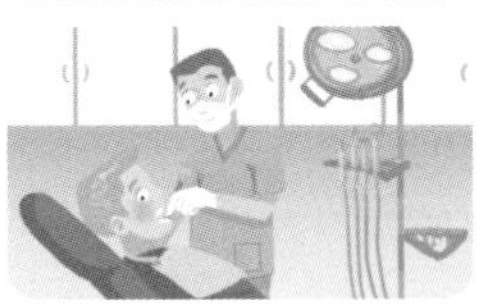 ______________________________ ______________________________ 

**3** **Complete the sentences with the verbs. Use the past simple.**

be (x3) dance listen look play

The school party [1]__________ great. There [2]__________ a lot of pizza and fruit juice. We [3]__________ a lot of games and there [4]__________ prizes too! We [5]__________ to pop music and our teacher [6]__________ with all the students – she [7]__________ very funny!

## 4 Write the adverbs.

1 loud ______ 2 bad ______ 3 quick ______
4 slow ______ 5 careful ______ 6 good ______

## 5 Write sentences about you using the adverbs from Exercise 4 and these adverbs of frequency.

always never often rarely sometimes usually

1 *I usually sing loudly.* (sing) 2 ______ (speak English)
3 ______ (walk) 4 ______ (run)
5 ______ (do my homework) 6 ______ (listen to my teacher)

## 6 Which is different? Circle. Then write sentences to say why.

1 ______ 2 ______ 3 ______

**I can ...**

| | Yes. | I need to practise. |
|---|---|---|
| • name different jobs and musical instruments. | ☐ | ☐ |
| • say what people do at their job. | ☐ | ☐ |
| • say how people do things and how often. | ☐ | ☐ |
| • talk about what I do every day and what I'm doing now. | ☐ | ☐ |
| • ask about actions in the past using *Did you ...?* | ☐ | ☐ |
| • write about a film or a play I watched. | ☐ | ☐ |

UNIT

# 3 Let's celebrate!

LESSON

## 1 Words

**1 Look and write. Use words from the two boxes.**

| eat | give | make |
|---|---|---|
| play | put up | see |
| throw | wear | |

| a costume | decorations | a parade |
|---|---|---|
| party games | presents | special food |
| streamers | traditional food | |

1 ______________

2 ______________

3 ______________

4 ______________

5 ______________

6 ______________

7 ______________

8 ______________

**2 How do people celebrate in these months? Listen and match.** TR: 10

1 January
2 June
3 July
4 December

A wear a costume
B eat traditional food
C play party games
D see a parade
E give presents
F put up decorations
G make special food

**3 Complete these sentences.**

1 When we celebrate ______________, we usually ______________.
2 When we celebrate ______________, we sometimes ______________.
3 My favourite day to celebrate is ______________. On this day, ______________.

# Grammar

*See page 124.*

## 1 Complete the text with these verbs. Use the past simple.

eat give go have play put up see

On Wednesday, I [1]_______________ flower decorations for Tết, the New Year celebration here in Vietnam. Thursday was the first day of Tết. My parents and grandparents [2]_______________ me some money. Then we [3]_______________ a special rice cake. Yum! Yesterday was Friday, the second day of Tết. We [4]_______________ a parade in the street and then we [5]_______________ to my aunt and uncle's house. We [6]_______________ a nice dinner there and after that we [7]_______________ games together.

**Lam, Vietnam**

## 2 Write sentences in the past simple.

| | | | |
|---|---|---|---|
| 1 | Lam / see | her cousin Tuan ✓ | her cousin Minh ✗ |
| 2 | Lam and Tuan / throw | streamers ✗ | a ball in the garden ✓ |
| 3 | Lam / wear | old clothes ✗ | new clothes ✓ |
| 4 | Lam and her mother / make | the rice cake ✓ | the dinner on Friday ✗ |

1 *Lam saw her cousin Tuan. She didn't see her cousin Minh.*
2 _______________
3 _______________
4 _______________

## 3 Write questions. Use the past simple.

1 you / put up / any decorations / last year? _______________
2 your parents / give / you / a present / last month? _______________
3 you / play / any games / last week? _______________
4 your dad / make / dinner / yesterday? _______________
5 you / throw / any streamers / last year? _______________

## 4 Answer the questions in Exercise 3 for you.

1 *Yes, I did. I put up decorations for our winter festival.*
2 _______________
3 _______________
4 _______________
5 _______________

LESSON 3
# Reading

## 1 Complete the sentences with the verbs. Use the past simple.

buy choose drink learn take

1 At the Pizza Festival in Naples, we ______________ how to make a great pizza.
2 I ______________ photos of some of the pizza makers.
3 Mum ______________ us pizzas in the market. They were only €3 each.
4 I ______________ a pizza with pieces of Italian cheese on it and it was delicious.
5 I ______________ a glass of juice with my food.

## 2 Read. Who said what? Write M (Mica) or A (Anna).

**Wonderful food festivals in Italy**

MICA
**Where did you go?**
We went to Florence in May. We went to the Ice Cream Festival!
**What did you do?**

ANNA
**Where did you go?**
We went to Perugia in October. We went to the Chocolate Festival.
**What did you do?**

☐ 1 At the Chocolate Museum, we learnt about how people make chocolate.
☐ 2 On the first day, we watched people on the street. They made sculptures from huge pieces of chocolate. They were beautiful and we ate some of the chocolate too!
☐ 3 At the end of the festival, we took photos with the ice cream makers.
☐ 4 The festival was in a big square on a hill. We bought a ticket and walked around the festival. We ate many different flavours of ice cream. One was milk, honey and rice flavour, but my favourite was orange, lemon and mint.
☐ 5 The next day, we drank some delicious hot chocolate.
☐ 6 People chose their favourite ice cream flavour to see who was the best ice cream maker.

## 3 Read again. Answer the questions.

1 In which city was the Ice Cream Festival? ______________
2 Where in the city was the Ice Cream Festival? ______________
3 Where did Mica and his family walk? ______________
4 When was the Chocolate Festival? ______________
5 Who did Anna watch on the first day? ______________
6 What did the people use to make the sculptures? ______________

LESSON 4

# Grammar

See page 124.

## 1 Complete the questions. Use the past simple. Then listen and write T (true) or F (false). TR: 11

1 **A:** Where ________ over the weekend?
**B:** I went to the orange festival. _____

2 **A:** What ____________ at the festival?
**B:** We did a lot of things. _____

3 **A:** When ____________ a parade?
**B:** We saw it in the afternoon. _____

4 **A:** What ____________ at the market?
**B:** We bought some lemons. _____

5 **A:** How many bottles of lemonade ____________ ?
**B:** I drank two bottles. _____

## 2 Write questions. Use the past simple. Then listen again and answer. TR: 12

1 how / Florian / go / to Menton
______________________________?
______________________________

2 how / people / make / the statues
______________________________?
______________________________

3 what / Florian / see / in the parade?
______________________________?
______________________________

4 where / Florian's family / go shopping
______________________________?
______________________________

5 why / Florian / drink / a lot of lemonade
______________________________?
______________________________

## 3 Imagine your friend went to this balloon festival. Write questions to ask your friend. Use the past simple and these words. Then write his/her answers.

how   how many   what   when   where   why

1 ______________________________?
______________________________

2 ______________________________?
______________________________

3 ______________________________?
______________________________

4 ______________________________?
______________________________

LESSON 5

# Writing An email

## 1 Read and put the sentences in order.

My day at the Maralal camel festival was great.

☐ Then, we watched a short camel race. The riders weren't very good and lots of the camels walked.

☐ First of all, we saw some amazing dancers.

☐ At the end, people gave money to the riders of the fastest camels.

☐ After the short camel race, there was a longer race. The riders were fantastic and the camels were very fast.

## 2 Complete the text with the underlined time connectors from Exercise 1.

Yesterday was my village's summer festival. [1] ______________ , we put up blue and white decorations. [2] ______________ , we wore blue clothes and flowers in our hair for a special dance in the square. [3] ______________ the dance, we had a big lunch with everyone in the village. [4] ______________ , there was more music and dancing. I had a great day!

## 3 Answer the questions about a celebration in your country last year.

1 What was the celebration? ______________________________

2 Where was it? ______________________________

3 What did people see or do?
- ______________________________
- ______________________________
- ______________________________
- ______________________________

4 Did people have fun? ______________________________

## 4 Write an email to a friend about the celebration in Exercise 3.

From: ______________

To: ______________

Subject: ______________

Hello ______________ ,

How are you? Yesterday was ______________________________ in ______________________________ . First of all, ______________________________ . Then, ______________________________ .

After ________ , ______________________________ .

At the end, ______________________________ .

People ______________ fun!

See you soon!

______________

VALUE Be a good neighbour.

## 1 Which children are good neighbours? Look and circle.

## 2 Read and circle the best answers for you.

1 There are a lot of flats in the same building. A good neighbour …
**A** bounces balls on the floor above another flat.
**B** plays music quietly.
**C** closes doors quietly.

2 An old person in the neighbourhood hasn't got any family. A good neighbour …
**A** sometimes visits the person.
**B** sometimes goes shopping for the person.
**C** never talks to the person.

3 A family in the neighbourhood has got a new baby. A good neighbour …
**A** is angry because the baby cries at night. **B** helps the family. **C** gives the baby a present.

4 A family is on holiday. A good neighbour …
**A** feeds their cat. **B** lives in their house. **C** waters their plants.

## 3 Do something nice for a neighbour. Then answer these questions.

1 What did you do for your neighbour? ______________________________
2 How did it make you feel? ______________________________
3 How did it make your neighbour feel? ______________________________

# UNIT 4 Sport for all

## LESSON 1 Words

### 1 Look and put the letters in order.

1 
lsatihetc
*athletics*

2 
flog
____________

3 
gnycasmtis
____________

4 
yellollbva
____________

5 
gynclic
____________

6 
vinigd
____________

7 
cei kantigs
____________

8 
orgwin
____________

9 
iginsal
____________

10 
sordowbinnag
____________

### 2 Read and write the words from Exercise 1.

In this sport:

1 you race and jump on snow. ____________
2 you race in boats. ____________ , ____________
3 you run in races, you jump or throw. ____________
4 you race on bikes. ____________
5 you hit a ball. ____________ , ____________
6 you jump into water. ____________
7 you dance or race on ice. ____________
8 you do activities on the floor and in the air. ____________

### 3 Listen to a conversation about the Paralympic Games. Circle the correct answer. TR: 13

1 *Ice skating / Snowboarding* is a sport in the Winter Paralympics.
2 In sitting volleyball, you sit *in special chairs / on the floor.*
3 The girl and her father can see *sailing / rowing* races in the Summer Paralympics.
4 They *can / can't* see cycling and athletics races.
5 The girl wants to see *two / three* sports at the Paralympics.

# Grammar

See page 125.

## 1 Read about a skier. Complete the text with *can, can't, could* or *couldn't*.

Cristian Ribera is from Brazil. He [1] *can't* walk, but he [2] __________ do lots of sports today. When he was a young boy, he [3] __________ do cool tricks on his skateboard and he [4] __________ swim very quickly in a swimming pool too. But he [5] __________ ski and he wanted to change that. When he was 12, he took his first skiing lesson, on special skis called 'sit-skis'. Soon he [6] __________ ski very well and Brazil chose him for the Paralympic ski team. At the age of 15, he raced in the Winter Paralympic Games. He was the youngest athlete there!

## 2 Listen to a conversation about Cristian Ribera. Answer the questions. TR: 14

1 Could Cristian practise skiing on snow in Brazil?

______________________________

2 Can people ski in South America?

______________________________

3 Where could Cristian do his kind of skiing?

______________________________

4 Could Cristian practise in Europe often?

______________________________

5 Could Cristian practise on roads?

______________________________

6 Can Cristian race in the Paralympics next year?

______________________________

## 3 Complete these sentences about you. Use *can, can't, could* and *couldn't*.

1 When I was a baby, I *could cry*, but I *couldn't talk*. I __________, but I __________.

2 Before I started school, I __________, but I __________. I __________, but I __________.

3 Now I __________, but I __________. I __________, but I __________.

LESSON 3

# Reading

## 1 Complete the sentences with these words.

brave nervous surprised tired

1 People were ____________ when they saw Eric, because he swam slowly.
2 Olympic divers must be very ____________ because they dive from very high up.
3 All athletes feel ____________ before their race starts.
4 Athletes in long races feel very ____________ at the end.

## 2 Read and put the text in order.

### The Olympic dream!

[ ] **A** After the race, Eric was a hero. His time was very slow, but it didn't matter. People thought he was very brave.

[ ] **B** Eric only started swimming in January 2000. He was 21 years old. He practised in a small swimming pool in a hotel. When he saw the Olympic pool in Sydney, he was surprised. It was huge! It was 50 metres long. He couldn't see the other end of it! The pool at home was only 12 metres long.

[ ] **C** In 2016, Eric went to the Olympics in Rio de Janeiro, Brazil. He didn't swim for Equatorial Guinea. He was the team's coach!

[ ] **D** In Eric's race, there were two other swimmers. But they both jumped in the pool too early and the referee stopped the race. When the race started again, Eric was the only swimmer and he was nervous. Everyone watched him. He started to swim very quickly, but soon he felt very tired. The crowd cheered 'Eric! Eric!' This helped him to finish.

[1] **E** Eric Moussambani was a star at the Olympics in Sydney in 2000. The swimmer from Equatorial Guinea didn't win a medal, but the crowd loved him.

## 3 Read again. Circle the correct answer.

1 Eric *won / didn't win* a swimming medal in the Olympics.
2 Eric was surprised because the swimming pool in Sydney was very *big / old*.
3 The race stopped because *Eric / the other swimmers* did something wrong.
4 Eric was *the only swimmer / one of three swimmers* to finish the race.
5 Eric was a hero because he was very *fast / brave*.
6 Eric *was a swimmer / helped other swimmers* in the 2016 Olympics.

## Grammar

See page 125.

### 1 Complete the table.

| Subject pronouns | Object pronouns |
|---|---|
| I | 1 ________ |
| you | 2 ________ |
| he | 3 ________ |
| she | 4 ________ |
| it | 5 ________ |
| we | 6 ________ |
| you | 7 ________ |
| they | 8 ________ |

### 2 Read and circle the correct pronouns.

In the 1998 Olympics, Larry Lamieux was in a sailing race when [1] *he / him* saw two men from a different race in the water. 'Help [2] *we / us*!' they shouted to [3] *he / him*. Larry stopped racing and helped [4] *they / them*. He didn't win a medal for the race, but he won another medal for being a hero.

In 2016, Abbey D'Agostino from the US and Nikki Hamblin from New Zealand were running in the Olympic 5000-metre race. But [5] *they / them* fell. Nikki was on her feet again quickly, but Abbey didn't move. Nikki helped [6] *she / her* to stand up. 'Finish the race with [7] *I / me*,' she said. They finished [8] *them / it* in last place, but they won a special prize for being kind.

### 3 Complete the sentences with object pronouns for the underlined words.

1 I help my brother in gymnastics and he helps ___*me*___ .
2 She went to Yuki's ice skating show, but Yuki didn't see ________ .
3 Stefan is a new boy on my team and I really like ________ .
4 You didn't win the race. I finished before ________ .
5 I play volleyball at school and I love ________ .
6 We have lessons with Mrs Peron and she's very kind to ________ .
7 Your snowboarding tricks are cool – you're really good at ________ !

# LESSON 5 **Writing** A factfile

## 1 Read and order the sentences about Wu Minxia, a diver from China.

- [ ] **A** When she was 18, she won her first Olympic gold medal.
- [ ] **B** When she was young, she liked watching diving on TV.
- [ ] **C** When she was 30, she won her seventh Olympic medal and her fifth Olympic gold.
- [ ] **D** When she was 15, she won the World Championships.
- [ ] **E** After her first Olympics, she had problems with her feet and often couldn't dive.

## 2 Underline the time phrases in Exercise 1.

## 3 Complete these sentences about you. Use *when*.

1 *When I was* ____________, I had my first ____________ lesson.
2 ____________, I learnt to ____________ .
3 ____________, I went to ____________ .

## 4 Choose a famous athlete from your country. Find out about him/her and make notes.

name?
date of birth?
sport?
started (sport)?
joined (team)?
won Olympic medal?
nickname?
place of birth?
activities when young?
broke world record?
stopped (sport)?

## 5 Choose information from Exercise 4. Write a factfile about the athlete.

**Name:** ____________

____________ : ____________
____________ : ____________
____________ : ____________

When he/she was ____________, he/she ____________ .
When he/she ____________, ____________ .
When ____________, ____________ .
When ____________, ____________ .

VALUE Have fun doing sport.

## 1 Read and tick (✓) the best answers for you.

**1 Why do you do sport?**

- ☐ Because my parents and teachers say I have to.
- ☐ Because I want to be healthy.
- ☐ Because I want to win.
- ☐ Because I can do sport with my friends.

**2 When do you do sport?**

- ☐ Only at school.
- ☐ In the gym after school or at the weekend.
- ☐ In my free time with friends and family.
- ☐ Never.

**3 Which kinds of sport do you like?**

- ☐ Races.
- ☐ Games with a winner at the end.
- ☐ Games without a winner at the end.
- ☐ Sport that I can do without other people.

**4 What do you do when you win at a sport?**

- ☐ Laugh at the other people because they didn't win.
- ☐ Say 'good game' to the other people.
- ☐ Feel happy because everyone had fun.
- ☐ Stop playing other sports that I can't win at.

## 2 Circle the best answers.

1 *Try / Don't try* lots of different sports.
2 *Play / Don't play* sport with your friends.
3 *Laugh / Don't laugh* at other people when they don't win.
4 *Have / Don't have* fun when you're playing sport.
5 *Be / Don't be* sad when you don't win.

## 3 Complete this message to a friend.

Hi ____________________ !

Do you want to ________________________________________ with me?
It's a great sport because ________________________________________ .
We can meet at ________________________________________ o'clock at
________________________________________ .

What do you think?

Your friend, ____________________

# Game 1

**1** Listen, colour and write. TR: 15

**2** Write five sentences about the picture in Exercise 1.

1 ______________________________

2 ______________________________

3 ______________________________

4 ______________________________

5 ______________________________

## The tightrope across Niagara Falls

**1 Listen and number the words as you hear them. Then tell your partner how these words are related to the story.** TR: 16

carefully ☐ chair ☐ leg [1] loudly ☐ man ☐ potatoes ☐ quiet ☐

**2 Complete the story. Use the words from Exercise 1. There are two words you don't need.**

Charles Blondin was a famous tightrope walker. There are a lot of stories about him. People say he could stand on one [1]____________ in the middle of the tightrope and that he could sit on a [2]____________ . He was very brave and the crowd always cheered [3]____________ when they watched him walking on the tightrope.

One day, he asked the crowd, 'Do you think I can walk on the tightrope with [4]____________ in my wheelbarrow?'

Everyone shouted, 'Yes!'

But when Blondin asked who wanted to sit in the wheelbarrow, everyone was [5]____________ because they were scared.

**3 Tick (✓) the things you think are true if you want to be a tightrope walker.**

1 You have to be good at gymnastics. ☐
2 You have to be tall. ☐
3 You have to be brave. ☐
4 You have to wear a blindfold. ☐
5 You have to live near a waterfall. ☐

**4 Imagine you're going to be a tightrope walker in your town. Draw a picture and answer the questions.**

1 Where is the tightrope?

______________________________

2 How long is the tightrope?

______________________________

3 How high off the ground is the tightrope?

______________________________

4 How do you feel when you walk across the tightrope?

______________________________

# Review 2: Units 3–4

## 1 Circle seven sports.

canathleticsswisailingtbgolfdavolleyballbesdivingjucyclingmerowington

## 2 Complete the text with *can, can't, could* or *couldn't*.

Shaquille O'Neal was a famous basketball player, but he [1] __________ play basketball a lot now because he hurt his leg. His son, Shareef, [2] __________ play basketball well when he was a child, but he [3] __________ skateboard. He started to play basketball when he was 13. Later, he was very good and he [4] __________ play with his school team. Now he's 18, he [5] __________ play basketball at college and may be a professional player in the future, like his dad.

## 3 Look. Write sentences and questions.

| | |
|---|---|
| Carmen – buy pizza | ✓ |
| Tom – put up decorations | ✓ |
| Lisa – make a cake | ✗ |
| Dave – choose music | ✓ |
| Amy – bring party games | ✗ |
| Mark – throw streamers | ✓ |

1 What did Tom do?
____________________

2 What did Mark do?
____________________

3 What did Lisa do?
____________________

4 ____________________
She bought the pizza.

5 ____________________
He chose music.

6 ____________________
She didn't bring party games.

**4** **Look at the pictures and read the beginning of the story. Continue the story with your own ideas.**

1

Laura is having a party today. She invited her family and friends to celebrate. Dad's in the kitchen making a cake. Mikey's in the kitchen too.

2

______________________
______________________
______________________
______________________
______________________
______________________

3

______________________
______________________
______________________
______________________
______________________
______________________

4

______________________
______________________
______________________
______________________
______________________
______________________

**5** **Think about your last party. Complete the questions with object pronouns and answer them for you.**

1 When was your party? Where did you have ____________?

______________________________________________

2 Did your parents make a cake or special food? Did you help ____________?

______________________________________________

3 Did your friends come to your party? What presents did they give ____________?

______________________________________________

4 Did you listen to music? Who chose ____________?

______________________________________________

| **I can ...** | Yes. | I need to practise. |
|---|---|---|
| • say what people do at parties and name different sports. | ☐ | ☐ |
| • talk about actions in the past and ask questions. | ☐ | ☐ |
| • talk about ability now and in the past. | ☐ | ☐ |
| • use object pronouns. | ☐ | ☐ |
| • write an email to a friend and a factfile about an athlete. | ☐ | ☐ |

# UNIT 5 Incredible places

## LESSON 1 Words

### 1 Do the puzzle. What's the mystery word?

1 

2 

3 

4 

5 

6 

7 

8 

9 

10 

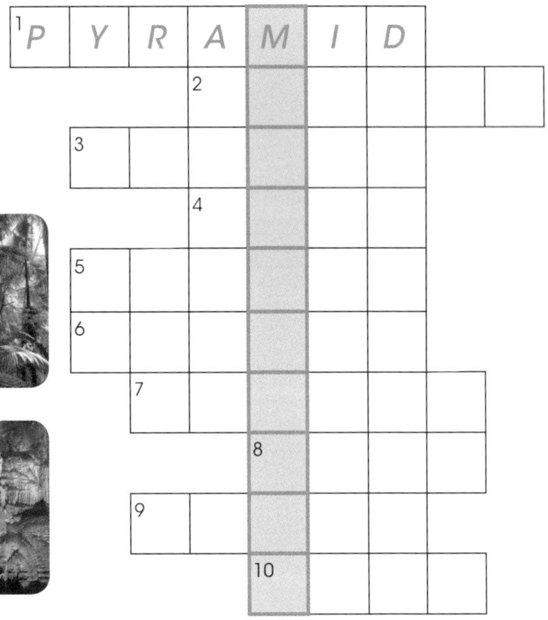


_______________ is an island and it's a country in Africa.

### 2 Write about you. Write words from Exercise 1 and your own ideas.

1 I often see ____________ and ____________ near my home.

2 I sometimes see ____________ and ____________ when I go on holiday.

3 One day, I want to go to ____________ because ______________________ .

4 I don't want to go to ____________ because ______________________ .

### 3 Listen to a girl talking to a friend about her holiday in Jamaica. Match. TR: 17

1 She went to a castle

2 She went to an island

3 She saw some birds

4 She saw a dolphin

5 She walked across a bridge

A on the rocks.

B in the waves.

C in the jungle.

D without any houses on it.

E above a cave.

# Grammar

LESSON 2

*See page 126.*

## 1 Read and circle the correct answer.

**JORDAN Where to go**

**Aqaba** is the [1] *better / best* place in Jordan for swimming and snorkelling. You can see beautiful fish there.

**Wadi Rum** is in the desert. Walking across its amazing rock bridge is one of the [2] *scarier / scariest* things to do in Jordan, but it's [3] *cooler / coolest* than any bridge in a city.

**Petra** is an ancient city in the pink rocks of the desert. It has some of Jordan's [4] *older / oldest* buildings.

**The Dead Sea** is Jordan's [5] *larger / largest* lake. Its water is [6] *saltier / saltiest* and [7] *worse / worst* to drink than sea water!

**Amman** is Jordan's [8] *bigger / biggest* city. It has great shops and the country's [9] *busier / busiest* markets.

## 2 Complete the sentences with the comparative and superlative forms of these adjectives.

bad dark easy far hot long nice

1 The ______________ places on Earth are in the desert, so drink a lot of water when you visit.
2 Mountains are always ______________ from the sea than beaches.
3 It's ______________ to swim in a swimming pool than in the sea because waves make swimming difficult.
4 Some people like snow. They think it's ______________ than rain.
5 When you're in a cave without a light, it's ______________ than at night.
6 The world's ______________ river is probably the Nile, but the Amazon is very long too.
7 One of the ______________ places in the world for plants is Antarctica. Almost nothing can grow there.

## 3 Write your own sentences using comparative or superlative forms.

1 sunny / country *Spain is a sunnier country than Ireland.*
2 big / city ______________
3 nice / beach ______________
4 good / shop ______________
5 tall / building ______________
6 rainy / month ______________

## LESSON 3 Reading

### 1 Read and circle the correct answers.

Like the Eiffel Tower in Paris, Burj Al Arab in Dubai is an [1] *important / exciting* symbol of its city. The restaurant on the 27$^{th}$ floor is very [2] *dangerous / popular* – everyone wants to eat there. Outside, on the roof of the building, there are sometimes [3] *exciting / dangerous* tennis or table-tennis matches between famous players. Brave athletes do [4] *popular / dangerous* things, for example, kitesurfing off the top of the building into the sea!

### 2 Read and complete with the correct form of these words. There are two words you don't need.

bad beach dive large rainy snow sport start up

**The desert sands!**

Dubai is the [1]____________ and most important city in the United Arab Emirates. Dubai is by the sea, but all the land around it is desert. Many people want to work and live there. The most popular place to live is by the [2]____________ . It is much cooler there. But there isn't much space to live by the beach any more. In 2001, people [3]____________ to build the Jumeirah Islands on the water. They used rocks and sand to make them. They look like palm trees!

Outside Dubai, there are huge hills of sand called 'dunes'. There are thousands of kilometres of them. There is an exciting [4]____________ you can do on them: sandboarding! This is the same as snowboarding, but it's on sand instead of [5]____________ ! It's a lot of fun, but you need to be careful too – it is dangerous to be in the hot sun for a long time. Drive [6]____________ to the top of the dunes, then sandboard down. The [7]____________ part is that you have to walk back up afterwards!

### 3 Answer the questions.

1 What kind of land is there around Dubai?

________________________________________

2 How did people build the Jumeirah Islands?

________________________________________

3 How is sandboarding different to snowboarding?

________________________________________

4 Why do you need to be careful when you are sandboarding?

________________________________________

5 What do you have to do after you sandboard down a dune?

________________________________________

## Grammar

LESSON 4

See page 126.

**1 Complete the sentences with the adjectives in brackets. Use the comparative or superlative form.**

1 The animals in Nepal are ______________ than the animals in Costa Rica. (interesting) ☐
2 Some of the ______________ mountains in the world are in Nepal. (famous) ☐
3 The mountains in Costa Rica are ______________ to climb than the mountains in Nepal. (difficult) ☐
4 The mountain views in Costa Rica are ______________ than the views in Nepal. (beautiful) ☐
5 The beach at Tamarindo is one of the ______________ in Costa Rica. (popular) ☐
6 Surfing is ______________ at Tamarindo than at other beaches. (exciting) ☐

**2 Listen to a boy comparing Costa Rica and Nepal. What does he think? Write T (true) or F (false) in the boxes in Exercise 1.** TR: 18

**3 Look at the three activities. Complete the sentences with your ideas and these adjectives. Use the comparative and superlative forms.**

| bad | boring | dangerous | difficult |
|---|---|---|---|
| exciting | expensive | good | interesting |

**Boat trip** See beautiful castles from a boat on the river.

**Snowboarding lesson**
Learn snowboarding in the mountains.

**Chocolate museum visit**
Learn about chocolate (and eat some too!).

1 The snowboarding lesson is ______________ than the boat trip.
2 The museum visit is ______________ than the snowboarding lesson.
3 The boat trip is ______________ than the museum visit.
4 I think the snowboarding lesson is the ______________ activity.
5 I think the ______________ is the ______________ activity.

LESSON 5

# Writing A travel brochure

## 1 Read. Underline the letters that should be capital letters.

M
madagascar is a beautiful island in the indian ocean. there are amazing animals in its deserts and jungles, and great museums and markets in its most important city, antananarivo. you can take a boat along the tsiribinha river and look for lemurs on the rocks. if you want to see baby lemurs, the best time to go is between october and december.

## 2 Answer these questions about your village, town or city.

1 What can you do there?

______________________________

2 When is the best time to go?

______________________________

3 How do you get there?

______________________________

4 What clothes do you need there?

______________________________

5 What other information about the place is important?

______________________________

6 How can you describe it using an adjective in the superlative form?

______________________________

## 3 Choose your best ideas from Exercise 2. Write a travel brochure for your village, town or city.

Visit ______________________________

In ______________, you can ______________

______________________________

______________________________

It ______________________________

**When to go:** ______________________________

**How to get there:** ______________________________

______________ : ______________

## VALUE Explore new places.

### 1 Read and tick (✓) the best answers for you.

**1** How many new places did you go to last year?
- ☐ None. I always go to the same places.
- ☐ Some, but not very many.
- ☐ Lots! I often go to new places on holiday and at the weekend.

**2** Do you like going to new places?
- ☐ No, I don't. It's boring to explore new places.
- ☐ Sometimes, but my favourite places are usually the places that I know well.
- ☐ Yes, I do. It's interesting to explore new places.

**3** How do you like to explore new places?
- ☐ On foot.
- ☐ By bike or boat.
- ☐ By car or bus.

**4** How do you find your way around when you're in a new place?
- ☐ I look at a map.
- ☐ I use the Internet.
- ☐ I ask other people.

### 2 Find out about a new place that you want to explore. Then answer the questions.

**1** What place do you want to explore? ______________________________

**2** How can you get there? ______________________________

**3** What do you want to see and do there? ______________________________

**4** Why did you choose this place? ______________________________

### 3 Draw a picture of yourself exploring the place in Exercise 2.

UNIT
# 6 Cool clothes

LESSON
## 1 Words

**1 Look and read. Write the correct words. There are two words you don't need.**

| a bracelet | comfortable | leggings | plain | a pocket |
|---|---|---|---|---|
| spotted | striped | sunglasses | trainers | |

1 You can carry keys and small toys in this part of your clothes. ______________

2 This is a design with lines of different colours. ______________

3 These clothes feel good when you wear them. ______________

4 You wear these to protect your eyes on sunny days. ______________

5 This describes something that is only one colour. ______________

6 You wear these on your feet when you play basketball or volleyball. ______________

7 You wear this around your hand/arm. ______________

**2 Listen, colour and write.** TR: 19

**3 Complete the sentences about you.**

1 I like wearing ______________ and ______________ .

2 I don't often wear ______________ .

3 I never wear ______________ .

4 I think ______________ clothes are better than ______________ .

5 My most comfortable clothes are my ______________ and my ______________ .

6 I usually have ______________ in my coat pocket.

# Grammar

See page 127.

## 1 Colour the words that can complete this question. What's the mystery picture?

Whose are these clothes? Are they ______________ ?

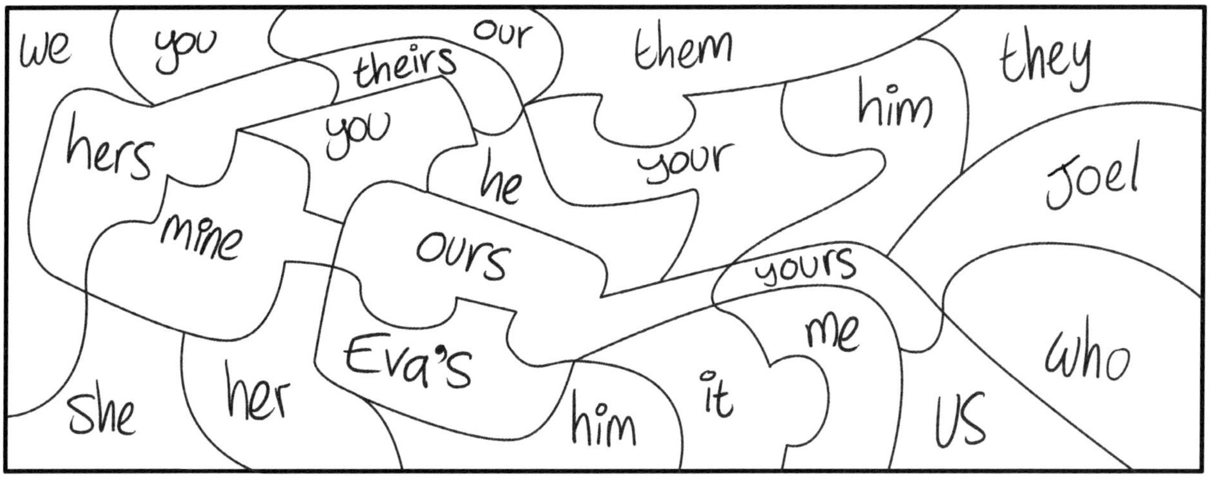


## 2 Complete the conversations with possessive pronouns.

1 **A:** Are those trainers David's?
**B:** Yes, I think they're ______________ .

2 **A:** Whose is that striped hat?
**B:** It's ______________ . I bought it last week.

3 **A:** I thought these sunglasses were Lucia's, but she says they're not ______________ . Are they ______________ ?
**B:** No, they aren't mine.

4 **A:** Wow! Whose big car is that?
**B:** It's ______________ . There are seven people in our family.

5 **A:** Is this Giorgia and Matteo's house?
**B:** No, that one's ______________ , opposite the café.

## 3 Answer the questions. Use possessive pronouns.

1 Our English book is green. What about yours? *Ours is* ______________

2 There are three people in my family. How many are there in yours?
______________

3 Our home is in Istanbul. What about yours? ______________

4 My grandma and grandpa's home is near ours. Where's your grandparents' home?
______________

5 My best friend's favourite sport is football. What's your best friend's favourite sport?
______________

LESSON 3

# Reading

## 1 Complete the text with these words.

frighten hurt match weak

The day after Odd Socks Day, our teacher asked us, 'What do superheroes do when bad people [1]____________ or [2]____________ others?' We talked about how we could be like superheroes and how we could keep everyone at our school safe and happy. We wore leggings and made masks to [3]____________ the colour of our leggings. We were all superheroes! And now we know: none of us are too small or too [4]____________ to stop bullying.

## 2 Read. Complete the text with the phrases (A–D).

**A** children who are different to them  
**B** we celebrated it at our school last week  
**C** why did we do it  
**D** all children are important

### Odd Socks Day

We usually wear socks to keep our feet warm. But socks can have a message too!

Who says your socks need to match? It was Odd Socks Day on Monday, 13th November and [1]____________ . We met in the playground at 8.45 before school started. Everyone wore different socks on each foot. It was a lot of fun, but [2]____________ ?

Well, all week we talked about bullying at school. A bully is a person who hurts or frightens other people. Older and stronger children sometimes bully the younger, weaker children, or [3]____________ . We want to stop bullying at our school. So, on Odd Socks Day, we wear different socks to show everyone that it is good to be different and that [4]____________ . Everyone needs to feel happy and safe at school.

Let's stop bullying!

## 3 Read again. Circle the correct answers.

1. Socks usually *have a message / keep feet warm.*
2. Odd Socks Day was *fun / boring.*
3. There was a special week at school about *socks / bullying.*
4. The message of Odd Socks Day is that *it's good to be different / socks are important.*
5. It's important that everyone feels *scared / safe* at school.

# Grammar

See page 127.

## 1 Complete the sentences with these words.

to buy to catch ~~to hold~~ to learn to make to play

1 I like having a pocket in my coat *to hold* my keys.
2 I walked to the bus stop ______ a bus.
3 I went to the shopping centre ______ some new trainers.
4 I needed the trainers ______ volleyball.
5 I'm on a volleyball team ______ new friends.
6 I practise volleyball every week ______ how to play better.

## 2 Mo Bridges makes bow ties. Listen and write T (true) or F (false). TR: 20

1 Mo chose his clothes to feel comfortable. ____
2 He went to the shop to look for his grandma. ____
3 Mo put photos of his bow ties on the Internet to sell them. ____
4 He went on TV to talk about his bow ties. ____
5 He went to the White House to give the president of the United States a bow tie. ____

Mo Bridges wearing one of his bow ties

## 3 Complete the sentences with your own ideas. Use infinitives of purpose.

1 People wear sun hats in summer *to keep their heads cool*.
2 People go to cafés ______.
3 People play sports ______.
4 I go to school ______.
5 I ______.
6 I ______.

# LESSON 5 **Writing** An invitation

**1 Read and complete the invitation with this information. Leave one space empty.**

2.00 pm    7    8th    11.00 am

Dear Carlo,
Please come to my party! It's a pool party, so bring your swimming costume.
**Date:** [1]_______________ July
**Place:** [2]_______________ Park Road [3]_______________ . My mum is going to drive us to the swimming pool.
**Time:** [4]_______________ to [5]_______________
We're going to have lunch at the swimming pool.
Please call 0785126956 to say if you can come.
Larissa

**2 Answer the questions.**

1. What date is your birthday? ____________________
2. What time do you start school? ____________________
3. What time do you finish school? ____________________
4. What's your address? ____________________

**3 Plan a school party for children and parents to celebrate the end of the school year. Write your ideas.**

- time (start and end)
- date and place
- activities
- how people can say if they can come
- what to bring/wear
- other important information

**4 Write an invitation to your party. Include the most important information from Exercise 3.**

Come to a party to ____________________.

____________________

____________________

We hope you can be there! ____________________

VALUE Look after your things.

**1** Which pictures show people looking after things? Look and tick (✓).

1 

☐

2  ☐

3  ☐

4  ☐

5  ☐

6  ☐

**2** Draw something that's special to you. Then answer the questions.

1 What is it?

______________________________

______________________________

2 Where did it come from?

______________________________

______________________________

3 Why is it special to you?

______________________________

______________________________

4 How do you look after it?

______________________________

______________________________

# Function 2: Going shopping

See page 128.

## 1 Look at the conversation. For each question, circle the correct answer. Then listen and check. TR: 21

1 **Shop assistant:** Hello. Can I help you?
**Customer:** **A** Yes, please. When is the party?
**B** Yes, please. I'm looking for a new skirt.
**C** I'm wearing a striped T-shirt.

2 **Shop assistant:** OK. What size are you?
**Customer:** **A** The skirt is for my sister and she's size 34.
**B** I want a red and blue skirt.
**C** That's very expensive!

3 **Shop assistant:** What colour do you want?
**Customer:** **A** I don't like it.
**B** Blue and white – they're my sister's favourite colours.
**C** Perfect! My sister loves skirts!

4 **Shop assistant:** Here's a nice skirt. Do you like it?
**Customer:** **A** I'm a size 34. How much is it?
**B** It's a blue coat.
**C** It's perfect! How much is it?

5 **Shop assistant:** It's 25 euros.
**Customer:** **A** Oh, that's very big!
**B** It's very cold.
**C** I'll take it!

## 2 Complete the conversation.

**A:** Hello. 1 ______________________________
**B:** Yes, please. I'm looking for a new coat.
**A:** 2 ______________________________
**B:** Green or black, please.
**A:** 3 ______________________________
**B:** I'm usually a medium.
**A:** Here you are.
**B:** Ooh, I like it. It's very nice.
4 ______________________________
**A:** It's 79 euros.
**B:** 5 ______________________________

## 3 Read and write a conversation.

You want to buy a new hat for your grandfather. His favourite colour is orange and he's got a big head!

# School trip 2: Hang Son Doong

## 1 Look and write the words.

cave clouds jungle river rocks stalactites stalagmites sunlight

1 

2 

3 

4 

5 

6 

7 

8 

## 2 Look at Student's Book page 66. Circle the correct answer.

1 How long is the cave?
   A 3 kilometres long  B 4 kilometres long  C 5 kilometres long
2 How can plants grow in the cave?
   A People plant them.  B There's sunlight.  C They grow near the river.
3 What are the stalagmites in the cave made of?
   A rock  B water  C sand
4 How tall are the largest stalagmites in the cave?
   A 7 metres tall  B 17 metres tall  C 70 metres tall

## 3 Imagine you visited Hang Son Doong cave in Vietnam. Write a postcard to your friend to tell him/her about the trip and what you saw.

# Review 3: Units 5–6

## 1 Read and complete the crossword.

1 Kings and queens lived here.
2 The Amazon rain forest is this.
3 ➔ It's green and it's got leaves.
3 ↓ It looks like a triangle.
4 There's a lot of sand and no water here.
5 It goes over a river.
6 It looks like a very big stone.
7 You can walk inside it. Bats live there.
8 There's water around it.
9 It starts in the sea and it moves to the beach.

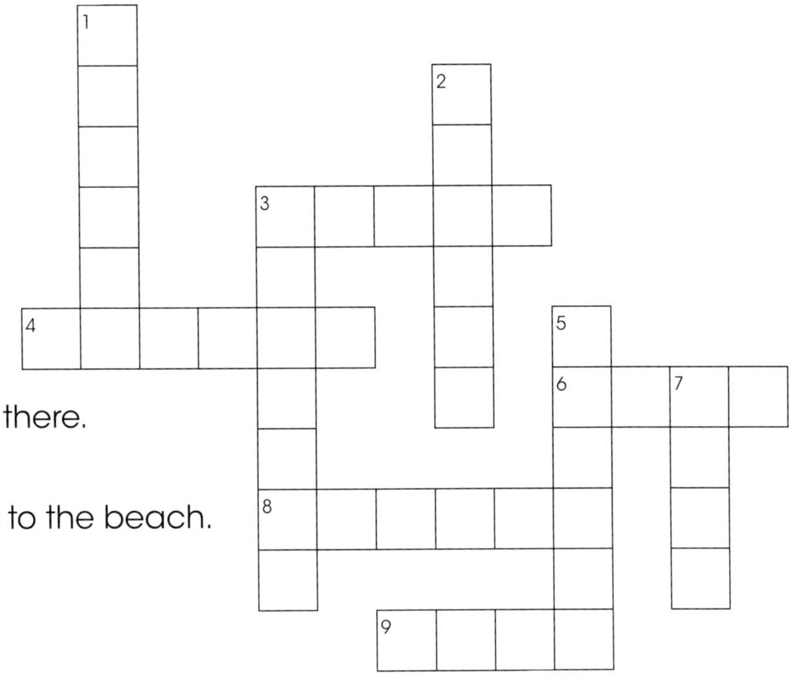


## 2 Read, choose and write.

dangerous    desert    popular    pyramid    striped    trainers

1 These are shoes you wear to do sport. ____________
2 This is a building you can see in Egypt. ____________
3 Zebras and tigers have this pattern. ____________
4 This place is very hot and it doesn't usually rain here. ____________
5 This is what something is when lots of people like it. ____________
6 Animals like lions and sharks are this. ____________

## 3 Whose clothes are these? Listen and write a letter in each box. TR: 22

1 Dad ☐    2 Mary ☐    3 Susan ☐    4 Tom ☐

A

B
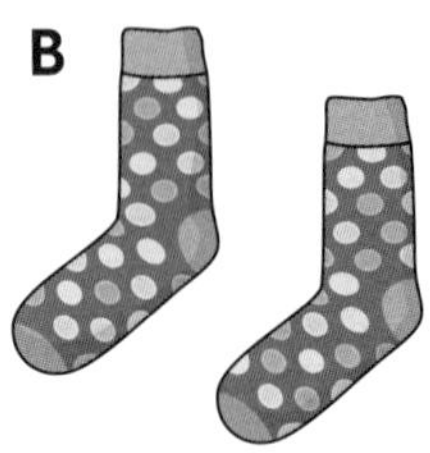
C

D

E

F

## 4 Answer the questions with your own ideas. Use infinitives of purpose.

1 Why do some people wear odd socks?

_______________

2 Why do people wear trainers when they do sport?

_______________

3 Why do people wear sunglasses? _______________

4 Why do clothes have pockets? _______________

## 5 Answer the questions about where you live.

1 What's the tallest building?

_______________

2 What's the most popular place to visit?

_______________

3 Who lives closest to the school?

_______________

4 What are the best and worst things about it?

_______________

## 6 Write sentences to compare where you live to other places in your country. Use these adjectives.

big busy exciting good hot interesting

_______________

_______________

_______________

_______________

| **I can ...** | Yes. | I need to practise. |
|---|---|---|
| • talk about interesting places and clothes. | ☐ | ☐ |
| • compare different things. | ☐ | ☐ |
| • talk about why people do things. | ☐ | ☐ |
| • use possessive pronouns. | ☐ | ☐ |
| • use capital letters correctly. | ☐ | ☐ |
| • write an invitation and a travel brochure. | ☐ | ☐ |

UNIT 1

# Grammar

## Lesson 2 Present simple and present continuous

| Present simple | Present continuous |
|---|---|
| Use the present simple form of a verb for things we do all the time. | Use the present continuous for things that are happening now. |
| Add *-s* when you use *he*, *she* or *it*. Use *don't* or *doesn't* to make a negative sentence. | Use *am*, *is* or *are*, and add *-ing* to the base form of the verb. |
| Use time expressions like *every day*, *on Mondays*, etc. | Use time expressions like *today*, *right now*, etc. |
| She **plays** football.<br>They **don't go** to school **on Saturday**. | I'**m playing** football **right now**.<br>They **aren't** (are not) **having** a snack. |

### Complete the sentences. Use the present simple or present continuous.

1 We ______________ in the classroom right now. (sit)
2 The boy ______________ football every day after school. (play)
3 She ______________ in the city right now. (not live)
4 They ______________ films at the weekend. (watch)
5 I ______________ today. (not read)

## Lesson 4 Adverbs of frequency

| *always* | *usually* | *often* | *sometimes* | *rarely* | *never* |
|---|---|---|---|---|---|

Use adverbs of frequency after the verb *to be*. Use them before other verbs.
When we ask questions, the adverb of frequency goes after the subject.

I'm **usually** happy.
We **usually** watch TV in the evening.
Does your sister **often** play tennis?

### Put the words in order.

1 never / on Sunday / to school / we / go ______________
2 tired / she / always / in the evening / is ______________
3 visit / on Friday / they / their grandmother / rarely ______________
4 are / books / sometimes / to read / difficult ______________
5 listen to / you / after school / often / music / do ______________

## Lesson 2 Past simple: *be*

| | |
|---|---|
| Use the past simple to talk about what happened in the past. | I **was** tired yesterday.<br>They **were** in the park.<br>She **wasn't** happy after the party.<br>**Was** it difficult?<br>**Were** the students in the classroom? |
| Use *was* with *I, he, she* and *it*, and *were* with *we, you* and *they*. Add *not* to make a sentence negative. Change the word order to make a question. | |

## Past simple: regular verbs

| | |
|---|---|
| Add *-ed* to regular verbs for all subjects. Use *didn't* (*did not*) and the base form of the verb to make a negative. Use *did* and the base form in questions. | He **played** football on Saturday.<br>We **didn't watch** a film last night.<br>**Did** they **listen** to music yesterday? |

### Complete the sentences.

1 We ______________ basketball yesterday. (not play)
2 I ______________ at school at eight o'clock. (be)
3 ______________ the sandwiches delicious? (be)
4 ______________ you ______________ your grandmother at the weekend? (visit)
5 They ______________ a great film at the cinema. (watch)

## Lesson 4 Adverbs of manner

| | |
|---|---|
| Most adverbs of manner are regular. We form them by adding *-ly* to the adjective. | Some adverbs are irregular. |
| loud → loud**ly**    happy → happ**ily**<br>correct → correct**ly**    easy → eas**ily**<br>careful → careful**ly** | good → **well**    hard → **hard**<br>fast → **fast** |
| He played the drums **loudly**.<br>They answered the questions **correctly**.<br>She did her homework **carefully**. | She swims **well**.<br>The dog runs **fast**.<br>She's a teacher and she works really **hard**. |

### Complete the sentences with the adverbs.

1 We play football ______________ . (good)
2 She speaks ______________ . (fast)
3 The lions watched the zebras ______________ . (quiet)
4 They danced ______________ . (happy)
5 He plays the guitar ______________ . (careful)

UNIT 3

# Grammar

## Lesson 2 Past simple: irregular verbs

| Some verbs have an irregular past simple (see the inside back cover for a list). The form of the verb is the same for all subjects and we form the negative and questions in the same way as the regular past simple verbs. | eat → They **ate** a big pizza last night.<br>throw → She **threw** the ball quickly.<br>buy → I **didn't buy** the book yesterday.<br>put → Did you **put** the book on the shelf? |
|---|---|

### Make sentences about last weekend. Use the past simple.

1 *On Saturday evening, I didn't eat chicken. I ate fish.* (eat)
2 ______________________________ (go)
3 ______________________________ (have)
4 ______________________________ (make)
5 ______________________________ (see)
6 ______________________________ (wear)

## Lesson 4 Past simple: *Wh-* questions

Use *did* + the base form of the verb to make *Wh-* questions with regular and irregular verbs.

Use *was* / *were* to make *Wh-* questions with *be*.

| What **did** you **eat** on Saturday? | When **was** the party? |
|---|---|
| Where **did** they **play** basketball? | Why **were** you late? |

### Write the questions.

1 When ______________________________?
We went to the park on Friday.

2 Why ______________________________?
We went to the park because it was sunny.

3 What ______________________________?
We ate sandwiches.

4 Who ______________________________?
My brother and his friends were at the park.

5 What ______________________________?
We watched the ducks on the lake.

## Lesson 2 *Can* and *could*

*Can* and *could* are modal verbs. Use *can* to talk about ability in the present.
Use *could* to talk about ability in the past.

Use the same form of *can/could* for all subjects and the base form of the verb.
Add *not* to make a negative sentence. Change the word order to make a question.

| | |
|---|---|
| We **can swim** fast.<br>She **can't play** basketball.<br>**Can** you **play** football well? | We **could ride** our bikes when we were three.<br>She **couldn't walk** when she was six months old.<br>**Could** you **play** golf when you were five? |

### Write sentences about your family and friends.

1 sister / play golf / ten — *My sister could play golf when she was ten.*
2 mum / ride a bike / four ______
3 dad / swim fast / now ______
4 cousins / speak English / twelve ______
5 I / drive a car / now ______
6 friends / play basketball well / now ______

## Lesson 4 Object pronouns

Use object pronouns to replace the object in a sentence when we don't want to repeat it.

| Subject pronoun | Object pronoun | Subject pronoun | Object pronoun | Subject pronoun | Object pronoun |
|---|---|---|---|---|---|
| I | me | she | her | they | them |
| you | you | it | it | | |
| he | him | we | us | | |

**The girl** threw the ball to the boy. He threw the ball back to **her**.
We saw **you**. Did you see **us**?

### Complete the sentences.

1 When you see Anna, can you give ______ this book?
2 I waved at my friend, but he didn't see ______ .
3 We ate a lot of the cake, but we didn't finish ______ .
4 Are you going to the beach? Can I go with ______ ?
5 My sister really likes animated films, but I don't like ______ .

UNIT 5

# Grammar

## Lesson 2 Comparatives and superlatives

We use a comparative adjective and *than* to compare two things.
We use *the* and a superlative adjective when something is at an extreme.

| Adjective | Comparative | Superlative | Some adjectives are irregular. | | |
|---|---|---|---|---|---|
| tall | tall**er than** | **the** tall**est** | **Adjective** | **Comparative** | **Superlative** |
| big | big**ger than** | **the** big**gest** | good | **better than** | **the best** |
| large | large**r than** | **the** large**st** | bad | **worse than** | **the worst** |
| busy | bus**ier than** | **the** bus**iest** | far | **further than** | **the furthest** |

A city is **larger than** a town. The Burj Khalifa is **the tallest** building in the world.

### Complete the sentences. Use comparatives and superlatives.

1 Canada is ______________ Greece, but China is ______________ country. (big)
2 Dad is ______________ me, but my grandma is ______________ person in our family. (old)
3 Spain is ______________ Ireland, but Saudi Arabia is ______________ . (hot)
4 Second place is ______________ third place, but coming in first is ______________ . (good)
5 My little brother is ______________ me, but my sister is ______________ . (naughty)

## Lesson 4 Comparatives and superlatives: long adjectives

An adjective is long when it has three or more syllables (*difficult, beautiful*), or when it has two syllables but doesn't end in *-y* (*famous, boring*). With these adjectives, use *more … than* and *the most* to make the comparative and superlative.

| Adjective | Comparative | Superlative |
|---|---|---|
| interesting | **more interesting than** | **the most interesting** |
| boring | **more boring than** | **the most boring** |

In some countries, basketball is **more popular than** volleyball.
The Eiffel Tower in Paris is one of **the most famous** buildings in the world.

### Make sentences. Use the comparative or superlative.

1 expensive (place in the town) *The cinema is more expensive than the café.*
2 dangerous (animal) *Sharks are the most dangerous animals in the sea.*
3 boring (free-time activity) ______________
4 exciting (film) ______________
5 difficult (school subject) ______________

## Lesson 2 Possessive pronouns

| Use possessive pronouns so you don't repeat the object. Use the same possessive pronoun for singular and plural nouns. | **Possessive adjective** | **Possessive pronoun** | **Possessive adjective** | **Possessive pronoun** |
|---|---|---|---|---|
| | my | mine | her | hers |
| | your | yours | our | ours |
| | his | his | their | theirs |

Whose is the blue jacket over there? It's **hers**.

Whose are these bags? Are they your bags? Yes, they're **ours**.

It's my bag. It's **mine**.

They're my bracelets. They're **mine**.

### Complete the sentences.

1 Where is Miguel? Is this book _______________ ?
2 Those pencils aren't _______________ . My pencils are longer.
3 Whose coat is this? Celia, is it _______________ ?
4 We haven't got blue shoes. _______________ are green.
5 Can Lucy use your ruler? _______________ is at home.

## Lesson 4 Infinitive of purpose

| Use an infinitive of purpose to say why we do something. The infinitive of purpose has the same form for all subjects. | I need to go to the library **to get** a book for my project.<br>We go to the dentist **to keep** our teeth healthy. |
|---|---|

### Match the questions and answers.

1 Why do we go to school?
2 Why do we do sport?
3 Why do people go to the beach?
4 Why do we wear shoes?
5 Why do people have mobile phones?

A To stay healthy.
B To protect our feet.
C To call friends or find information.
D To learn new things.
E To relax or swim in the sea.

# Functions

## Function 1: Giving directions

**Where** is your house?
**Go straight on.**
**Turn left** (at the end of the road).
**Turn right** (at the supermarket).
The school is **on the right**.

## Function 2: Going shopping

| | |
|---|---|
| Can I help you? | Yes, please. |
| **I'm looking for** a striped shirt. | |
| **How much is** this jacket? | **It's** 120 euros. |
| **What size are you?** | Small./Medium./Large. |
| **Here's a** lovely dress. | **I'll take** it! |

**Unit 1**
actor
animation
clown
dentist
designer
film director
firefighter
model
nurse
photographer
pilot
police officer
waiter

**Unit 2**
bang
carry
cello
classical music
climb
concert
dancer
drums
flute
keyboard
pop music
shout
singer
violin

**Unit 3**
buy – bought
choose – chose
drink – drank
eat traditional food
give presents
learn – learnt
make special food
play party games
put up decorations
see a parade
take – took
throw streamers
wear a costume

**Unit 4**
athletics
brave
cycling
diving
golf
gymnastics
ice skating
nervous
rowing
sailing
snowboarding
surprised
tired
volleyball

# Wordlist

**Unit 5**
bridge
castle
cave
dangerous
desert
exciting
important
island
jungle
plant
popular
pyramid
rock
wave

**Unit 6**
bracelet
comfortable
frighten
hurt
leggings
match
plain
pocket
spotted
striped
sunglasses
trainers
weaker

# Irregular verb list

| Infinitive | Past simple | Past participle |
|---|---|---|
| become | became | become |
| break | broke | broken |
| bring | brought | brought |
| build | built | built |
| burn | burnt/burned | burnt/burned |
| buy | bought | bought |
| catch | caught | caught |
| choose | chose | chosen |
| come | came | come |
| do | did | done |
| draw | drew | drawn |
| dream | dreamt/dreamed | dreamt/dreamed |
| drink | drank | drunk |
| drive | drove | driven |
| eat | ate | eaten |
| fall | fell | fallen |
| feed | fed | fed |
| find | found | found |
| fly | flew | flown |
| get | got | got |
| give | gave | given |
| go | went | gone |
| grow | grew | grown |
| have | had | had |
| hide | hid | hidden |
| hit | hit | hit |
| hold | held | held |
| hurt | hurt | hurt |
| know | knew | known |
| learn | learnt/learned | learnt/learned |
| leave | left | left |
| make | made | made |
| put | put | put |
| read | read | read |
| run | ran | run |
| say | said | said |
| stand | stood | stood |
| think | thought | thought |
| wake | woke | woken |
| write | wrote | written |

Thank you to the educators who provided invaluable feedback during the development of *Look*:

## CONSULTANTS

**Gabriela Klečková**, Teacher Trainer, University of West Bohemia, Czech Republic
**Luciana Fernández**, Teacher Trainer/Academic Consultant, ESSARP, Argentina
**Mari Nakamura**, Owner/Teacher Trainer/Teacher, English Square, Kanazawa
**Nguyen Quoc Hung, MA**, Teacher, Hanoi University, Hanoi
**Dr Sagrario Salaberri**, Professor, University of Almería, Spain

## ADVISORS

**Aisha Khawaja**, Early Childhood and EAL Specialist, GEMS Dubai American Academy, United Arab Emirates
**Alis Valenzuela**, Junior Manager, Children & Teenagers Program, Instituto Guatemalteco Americano (IGA), Guatemala
**Amanda Fonseca**, Academic Advisor, Brasil
**Andy Changan Li**, Teaching Director, Keyword Education, Shenzhen
**Carmen Virginia Pérez Cervantes**, Academic Director, La Salle México-Sur, México
**Emma Heyderman**, Director of Education, Lacunza - International House San Sebastian, Spain
**Jennifer Wu**, Vice President, American Eagle Institute, Taipei
**Julie Hwang**, Educational Consultant, Seoul
**Kevin McDonal, M.A.Ed.**, Curriculum Developer, Centro Cultural Costarricense-Norteamericano (CCCN), Costa Rica
**Maria-Araxi Sachpazian**, Managing Director, Input on Education, Greece
**Mayumi Tabuchi**, English Department Supervisor, Notre Dame Elementary School, Kyoto
**Paulo Rogerio Rodrigues**, Escola Mobile, Brasil
**Dr Stephen Louw**, Principle Trainer, Chichester College, Bangkok
**Streamline Language School**, Belarus
**Teresa Haeok Park**, Professor, International Graduate School of English (IGSE), Seoul

## REVIEWERS

### LATIN AMERICA

**André Hedlund**, Centro Cultural Brasil - Estados Unidos (CCBEU) - Goiânia, Brasil
**Dulce Stoll**, Colégio Miguel de Cervantes, Brasil
**Itana Lins**, Colégio Anchieta, Brasil
**Isabella Oliveira Campos Titoneli Alvim**, Instituto Brasil-Estados Unidos (IBEU) - Rio de Janeiro, Brasil
**Lorena Stern**, Colegio Madrid, México
**María Consuelo Velasco**, Colegio Santa Francisca Romana, Colombia
**Maria Eugenia Rodriguez**, Centro Cultural Salvadoreño Americano (CCSA), El Salvador
**Thays Ladosky**, Associação Brasil América (ABA) - Recife, Brasil
**Viviana María Valenti**, Universidad Nacional de Rosario, Argentina

### EUROPE

**Ainhoa Estella**, Simon Says, Spain
**Jennifer Chang**, A++ School, Spain
**Liana Boogaars**, Bilingual Kids, Netherlands
**Sandy Millin**, IH Bydgoszcz, Poland
**Shay Coyne**, Spain

### ASIA

**Fu Nuocheng**, 51 Talk, Beijing
**LV Yang**, 51 Talk, Beijing
**Wei Wang**, Beijing Haidian Teachers Training College, Beijing
**Su Jing**, Chencent Education, Beijing
**Rivers He**, Houhai Education, Beijing
**Junjun Guo**, Improve Education, Beijing
**Xu Huan**, New Oriental School, Beijing
**Wang Jing**, Rise Education, Beijing
**Song Haoyue**, TAL Education, Beijing
**Irene Chen**, Owen English, Chongqing
**Lily Ren**, Dalian Maple Leaf, Dalian
**Yuki Zheng**, Guangzhou Panyuzhixin Middle School, Guangzhou
**Rebecca Liu**, Hui Da Hai Wen Education, Guangzhou
**Nymark Wilkie**, Panyu Zhixin Zhongxue, Guangzhou
**Pingyuan Liu**, PTE Testing Center Guangzhou Office, Guangzhou
**Andrew W. Shewbart**, ALO7 Education, Shanghai
**Xiaofeng Shen**, DaDa, Shanghai
**Xiaobo Wang**, Only Education Group, Shanghai
**Liu Jun**, 3rd Stage, Shenzhen
**Katrina Li**, Acadsoc Limited, Shenzhen
**Fangfang Yan**, Keyword Education, Shenzhen
**Jinbo Shen**, Little Oxford Education, Shenzhen
**Natasa Natalie Radovanic**, Nankai Primary Shenzhen School, Shenzhen
**Keke Xu**, Xue Er Si, Shenzhen
**Monica**, Xue Er Si, Shenzhen
**Tanyuan Wang**, Freelance, Shenzhen
**Will Fu**, Aston English, Xian
**Wai Ling Nancy Chan**, Baptist Sha Tin Wai Lui Ming Choi Primary School, Hong Kong
**Dr Micaela de Senna Fernandes**, Centre for International Cooperation in Education, Macau
**Chloe Yu**, Chuan Kids, Taipei
**Steve Lambert**, Shane English School, Taipei
**Leonardo Tjen**, Teach Indonesia School, Jakarta
**Dr Tomohisa Machida**, Akita International University, Akita
**Ryan Hagglund**, MY English School, Higashine
**Marybeth Kamibeppu**, Hiroshima International School, Hiroshima
**Toshiyuki Niimura**, Kyoshin, Kawasaki
**Cynthia Akazawa**, Interact English School, Kurashiki
**Daniel Stoffers**, No Borders International School, Nagoya
**David Gonzales**, No Borders International School, Nagoya
**Kenn Gale**, No Borders International School, Nagoya
**Kori Herlein**, No Borders International School, Nagoya
**Michael Pettovello**, No Borders International School, Nagoya
**Chika Miyashita**, Joy World English Academy, Obihiro
**Eric Kane**, ELF Learning, Omihachiman
**Ai Murphy**, Murphy School of English, Onga
**Corazon Kato**, Chubu Gakuin University, Seki
**Dr Curtis Kelly**, Kansai University, Suita
**Nick Weston**, British Council Japan, Tokyo
**Leah Arai**, Kyoshin, Tokyo
**Reiko Hitomi**, Showa Elementary School, Tokyo
**Rie Hatai**, Showa Elementary School, Tokyo
**Chiyuki Yanase**, Sunny Field English, Tokyo
**Akiko Nagashima**, Tact Kodomomirai, Tokyo
**Rie Kobayashi**, Tact Kodomomirai, Tokyo
**Juwon Noh**, BCN Kids, Seoul
**Jinhee Lee**, YBM ECC, Seoul
**Tantiwa Neawjantuek**, Ban Kru Am, Ban Khoi
**Nguyen Thi Thu Phuong**, American English School (AMES), Hanoi
**Kathleen Steenkamp**, Apollo, Hanoi
**Zach Pinson**, Atlantic Education & Training, Hanoi
**Vu Thi Phuong Hien**, BINH MINH Group, Hanoi
**Do Thuy Duong**, IEG Global, Hanoi
**Tran Thanh Huyen**, Language Link, Hanoi
**Ann Brown**, Le Quy Don+VAS Hanoi, Hanoi
**Mitchell Baker**, Ocean Edu, Hanoi
**Nguyen Thi Huong**, Star Hanoi Primary School, Hanoi
**Tran Thi Thanh Phuc**, Vinschool, Hanoi
**Danh Nguyen**, AMA, Ho Chi Minh City
**Peter Waters**, Apollo, Ho Chi Minh City
**Giang Nguyen**, CEFALT, Ho Chi Minh City
**Malamatenia Gatsou**, ILA, Ho Chi Minh City
**Nguyen Thi Thanh Hien**, IPS, Ho Chi Minh City
**Nguyen Tri Nhu Quynh**, Pathway School, Ho Chi Minh City
**Trinh Thi Hoa My**, SEAMEO, Ho Chi Minh City
**Nguyen Thi Bao Khuyen**, Vietnam USA Society English Centers (VUS), Ho Chi Minh City
**Tran Thi Minh Nguyet**, Vietnam USA Society English Centers (VUS), Ho Chi Minh City
**Tran Ngoc Thuy Nhien**, Vinschool, Ho Chi Minh City
**Pham Huu Loc**, Vstar, Ho Chi Minh City
**Chris Nicholson**, Wellspring Saigon Int'l, Ho Chi Minh City
**Gia Linh Lam**, Yola, Ho Chi Minh City

# CREDITS

**STUDENT'S BOOK PHOTOS: 2** (t) © Teovel Iradon; (mt) © Emile Holba; (mmt) © Giacomo Checcucci; (mmb) © Jong-Won Heo/Getty Images; (mb) © Keith Ladzinski/Getty Images; (b) © aiqingwang/Getty Images; **3** (t) © Peter Zelei Images/Getty Images; (mt) © Johannes Schmitt-Tegge/AP Images; (mmt) © Diane Bondareff/AP Images; (mmb) © Vichaya Pop/500px; (mb) © spreephoto.de/Getty Images; (b) © Seah Poh Siang; **4–5** © Gabe DeWitt; **6–7** © AMI VITALE/National Geographic Creative; **9** © Teovel Iradon; **10** (tl) © Igor Bulgarin/Shutterstock.com; (tm) © Petrenko Andriy/Shutterstock.com; (tr) Hero Images Inc./Alamy Stock Photo; (ml) © ML Harris/Getty Images; (mm) © Maskot/Getty Images; (mr) © Maridav/Shutterstock.com; (bl) Hero Images Inc./Alamy Stock Photo; (bm) © Peter Dazeley/Getty Images; (br) © Schultheiss Selection GmbH & CoKG/Getty Images; **10–11** © Idaho Statesman/Getty Images; **12** © Hans Weise; **12–13** © Gavin Hellier/Getty Images; **14** © Martjn Kort; **15** © Anacleto Rapping/Getty Images; **16** © Tawatchai Prakobkit/EyeEm/Getty Images; **17** © Emile Holba; **18** (tl) © AVAVA/Shutterstock.com; (tml) © Jack.Q/Shutterstock.com; (tm) © PeopleImages/Getty Images; (tmr) © Blend Images - Mike Kemp/Getty Images; (tr) © Bill Reitzel/Getty Images; (bl) © Alenavlad/Shutterstock.com; (bml) © fitopardo.com/Getty Images; (bm) © Jim Dyson/Getty Images; (bmr) Craig Lovell/Eagle Visions Photography/Alamy Stock Photo; (br) © Aryan Firouzbakht Photography/Getty Images; **18–19** Gtres Información más Comuniación on line,S.L./Alamy Stock Photo; **20–21** © Souvid Datta; **22** © Kim Steele/Getty Images; **23** © Robin Marchant/Getty Images; **24** (l) PHILIPPE DAMONVILLE/Alamy Stock Photo; (tr) JASPERIMAGE/Alamy Stock Photo; (br) © neelsky/Shutterstock.com; **26–27** © Michael Nichols/National Geographic Creative; **29** © Giacomo Checcucci; **30** (tl) © Jupiterimages/Getty Images; (tm) © Hero Images/Getty Images; (tr) © Azami Adiputera/Shutterstock.com; (ml) © Sollina Images/Getty Images; (mm) © Sofie Delauw/Getty Images; (mr) © Tibor Bognar/Getty Images; (bl) © Dreet Production/Getty Images; (br) © Marc Romanelli/Getty Images; **30–31** © ED JONES/Getty Images; **32–33** © Bloomberg/Getty Images; **34** Tim Graham/Alamy Stock Photo; **35** © Ajit Solanki/AP Images; **36** (l) © The Asahi Shimbun/Getty Images; (tr) Jim West/Alamy Stock Photo; (br) © fdenb/Shutterstock.com; **37** © COPYRIGHT, Jong-Won Heo/Getty Images; **38** (tl) Elvele Images Limited/Alamy Stock Photo; (tml) markferguson2/Alamy Stock Photo; (tm) © CHRISTOF STACHE/Getty Images; (tmr) Nicolas RUNG/Alamy Stock Photo; (tr) © ElenaNichizhenova/Getty Images; (bl) © Tatyana Vyc/Shutterstock.com; (bml) © SolStock/Getty Images; (bm) © Onne van der Wal/Corbis Documentary/Getty Images; (bmr) © mbbirdy/Getty Images; (br) © miodrag ignjatovic/Getty Images; **38–39** © Alexandre Loureiro/Getty Images; **40–41** © Mike Powell/Getty Images; **41** © Professional Sport/Getty Images; **42** © Look Foto/Aurora Photos; **43** (t) PCN Photography/Alamy Stock Photo; (b) ZUMA Press Inc/Alamy Stock Photo; **44** © Stockforlife/Shutterstock.com; **45** (t) © Onne van der Wal/Corbis Documentary/Getty Images; (m) © Jupiterimages/Getty Images; (b) © Jack.Q/Shutterstock.com; **46–47** © Tony Bock/Getty Images; **48** (l) © miodrag ignjatovic/Getty Images; (ml) © CHRISTOF STACHE/Getty Images; (m) © Vadim Zakharishchev/Shutterstock.com; (mr) © SolStock/Getty Images; (r) Nicolas RUNG/Alamy Stock Photo; **49** © Keith Ladzinski/Getty Images; **50** (tl) © Shanshan0312/Shutterstock.com; (tml) © Pecold/Shutterstock.com; (tm) © David Ridley/Shutterstock.com; (tmr) © Krzysztof Bargiel/Shutterstock.com; (tr) © Dennis van de Water/Shutterstock.com; (bl) © Vixit/Shutterstock.com; (bml) © huyangshu/Shutterstock.com; (bm) © LexyK/Shutterstock.com; (bmr) © Sabine Hortebusch/Shutterstock.com; (br) © Brett Allen/Shutterstock.com; **50–51** © JoseIgnacioSoto/Getty Images; **52–53** © Andrey_Popov/Shutterstock.com; **53** © nodff/Shutterstock.com; **54** © Neale Clarke/Robert Harding; **55** © Laurent Bouvet/RAPSODIA/SuperStock; **56** (l) © DEA/PUBLIAER FOTO/Getty Images; (tr) © Andrey Armyagov/Shutterstock.com; (br) © aphotostory/Shutterstock.com; **57** © aiqingwang/Getty Images; **58–59** © guppyss/Shutterstock.com; **59** © Angela Lan; **60–61** © Helen Morgan School; **61** (tl) Radim Beznoska/Alamy Stock Photo; (tm) © DenisProduction.com/Shutterstock.com; (tr) © Chanita Chokchaikul/Shutterstock.com; (bl) © Ana_Sun/Shutterstock.com; (bm) Mint Images Limited/Alamy Stock Photo; (br) Juice Images/Alamy Stock Photo; **62** © Zen Sekizawa/Getty Images; **63** © Blend Images - KidStock/Getty Images; **64** (tl) © Ali Al Mubarak/Getty Images; (bl) Travel Pictures/Alamy Stock Photo; (r) © worradirek/Shutterstock.com; **66–67** © Ryan Deboodt; **68** (tl) © Beautiful landscape/Shutterstock.com; (tm) © Brett Allen/Shutterstock.com; (tr) © Pecold/Shutterstock.com; (bl) © Westend61/Getty Images; (bm) © LexyK/Shutterstock.com; (br) © Roy Toft/ National Geographic Creative.

**STUDENT'S BOOK ILLUSTRATIONS: 25** Brian Fitzgerald/Astound US; **27**, **67** Clive Goodyer/Beehive Illustration.

**WORKBOOK PHOTOS: 71** (tl) © mikkelwilliam/E+/Getty Images; (tm) © KidStock/Blend Images/SuperStock; (tr) © Reinhard Eisele/Mauritius/SuperStock; (ml) © Daniel Prudek/Shutterstock.com; (mm) © straga/Shutterstock.com; (mr) © Randi Scott/Shutterstock.com; (bl) © LukaM/Shutterstock.com; (bm) © stockcreations/Shutterstock.com; (br) © svariophoto/Shutterstock.com; **72** © PAUL NICKLEN; **74** (tl) © Maridav/Shutterstock.com; (tr) © Igor Bulgarin/Shutterstock.com; (ml) © Schultheiss Selection GmbH & CoKG/The Image Bank/Getty Images; (mr) © Maskot/Getty Images; (bl) © Maridav/Shutterstock.com; (br) © Petrenko Andriy/Shutterstock.com; **75** (tl) © DimaBerlin/Shutterstock.com; (tml) Vitalii Artiushenko/Alamy Stock Photo; (tmml) © Dmytro Gilitukha/Shutterstock.com; (tmmr) © Syda Productions/Shutterstock.com; (tmr) © Alexandros Michailidis/Shutterstock.com; (tr) Randy Duchaine/Alamy Stock Photo; (b) John Quixley - Australia/Alamy Stock Photo; **76** © Hans Weise; **78** © Rebecca Dickman; **80** (tl) © Jim Dyson/Getty Images Entertainment/Getty Images; (tm) © AVAVA/Shutterstock.com; (tr) © fitopardo.com/Moment/Getty Images; (mtl) © Bill Reitzel/DigitalVision/Getty Images; (mtm) Craig Lovell/Eagle Visions Photography/Alamy Stock Photo; (mtr) © Aryan Firouzbakht Photography/Moment/Getty Images; (mbl) © PeopleImages/DigitalVision/Getty Images; (mbm) © Blend Images - Mike Kemp/Brand X Pictures/Getty Images; (mbr) © Alenavlad/Shutterstock.com; (b) © TORU YAMANAKA/Staff/AFP Images/Getty Images; **81** (l) © KAZUHIRO NOGI/Staff/AFP Images/Getty Images; (m) © Atsuo Takanishi Lab, Waseda University, Tokyo, Japan; (r) © Associated Press; **82** © Souvid Datta; **83** (t) © Kokhanchikov/Shutterstock.com; (ml) © Hadrian/Shutterstock.com; (mm) © Studio CP/Getty Images; (mr) © Avigator Thailand/Shutterstock.com; (bl) © Sergey Ryzhov/Shutterstock.com; (bm) Cultura Creative (RF)/Alamy Stock Photo; (br) © Catherine Delahaye/Digital Vision/Getty Images; **84** (tl) Westend61 GmbH/Alamy Stock Photo; (tr) © Luis Molinero/Shutterstock.com; (bl) UpperCut Images/Alamy Stock Photo; (br) © Viorika/Getty Images; **87** (tl) © Independent birds/Shutterstock.com; (tml) © Soru Epotok/Shutterstock.com; (tmr) © Jatuporn Chainiramitkul/Shutterstock.com; (tr) © Twin Design/Shutterstock.com; (ml) © MOROZ NATALIYA/Shutterstock.com; (mml) © Serhii Brovko/Shutterstock.com; (mmr) © Peter Gudella/Shutterstock.com; (mr) © nampix/Shutterstock.com; (b) © Semeniaka Aleksandr/Shutterstock.com; **90** (tl) © Marc Romanelli/Blend Images/Getty Images; (tml) © Jupiterimages/Photolibrary/Getty Images; (tmr) © Hero Images/Getty Images; (tr) © Tibor Bognar/Corbis Documentary/Getty Images; (bl) © Sofie Delauw/Cultura/Getty Images; (bml) © Dreet Production/Alloy/Getty Images; (bmr) © Azami Adiputera/Shutterstock.com; (br) © Sollina Images/The Image Bank/Getty Images; **91** © vinhdav/Getty Images; **92** © Bloomberg/Getty Images; **93** (t) © AnnaBreit/Getty Images; (b) robertharding/Alamy Stock Photo; **94** GORAN TOMASEVIC/REUTERS/Newscom; **96** (tl) Elvele Images Limited/Alamy Stock Photo; (tml) Nicolas RUNG/Alamy Stock Photo; (tm) © ElenaNichizhenova/iStock/Getty Images; (tmr) miodrag ignjatovic/E+/Getty Images; (tr) markferguson2/Alamy Stock Photo; (bl) © CHRISTOF STACHE/AFP/Getty Images; (bml) © Tatyana Vyc/Shutterstock.com; (bm) © SolStock/E+/Getty Images; (bmr) © Onne van der Wal/Corbis Documentary/Getty Images; (br) © mbbirdy/iStock/Getty Images; **97** © Buda Mendes/Staff/Getty Images Sport/Getty Images; **98** © Mike Powell/Getty Images Sport/Getty Images; **99** (mr) © Photo by Chris Graythen/Getty Images Sport/Getty Images; **100** © Mark J. Terrill/AP/Shutterstock.com; **103** © Tony Bock/Toronto Star/Getty Images; **104** © Cassy Athena/ Contributor/Getty Images Entertainment/Getty Images; **106** (tl) © LexyK/Shutterstock.com; (tr) © Pecold/Shutterstock.com; (mtl) © Shanshan0312/Shutterstock.com; (mtm) © Brett Allen/Shutterstock.com; (mtr) © Dennis van de Water/Shutterstock.com; (mbl) © Krzysztof Bargiel/Shutterstock.com; (mbm) © Vixit/Shutterstock.com; (mbr) © David Ridley/Shutterstock.com; (bl) © huyangshu/Shutterstock.com; (br) © Sabine Hortebusch/Shutterstock.com; **107** © Nordicyigit/Shutterstock.com; **108** © nodff/Shutterstock.com; **109** (t) © Olga Danylenko/Shutterstock.com; (mt) © Parkol/Shutterstock.com; (mb) © yanik88/Shutterstock.com; (bl) © Matteo Colombo/Getty Images; (br) © Elan Fleisher/LOOK-foto/Getty Images; **110** © Lynn Gail/Lonely Planet Images/Getty Images; **115** © Giovanni Rufino/ Contributor/Disney ABC Television Group/Getty Images; **119** (tl) © Allgord/Shutterstock.com; (tml) © ThamKC/Shutterstock.com; (tmr) © Kevin Cox 1985/Shutterstock.com; (tr) © Vladimir Melnikov/Shutterstock.com; (bl) © Dennis van de Water/Shutterstock.com; (bml) © David Ridley/Shutterstock.com; (bmr) © Titus Group/Shutterstock.com; (br) © Lapis2380/Shutterstock.com.

**WORKBOOK ILLUSTRATIONS: 71**, **112** Amit Tayal/Beehive Illustration; **85**, **86**, **102**, **120** Angeles Peinador/Beehive Illustration; **88**, **89**, **105**, **117** Clonefront/Beehive Illustration; **95**, **113** Russ Daff/Beehive Illustration.

NATIONAL GEOGRAPHIC LEARNING

National Geographic Learning,
a Cengage Company

***Look 4A Combo Split***

Student's Book author: Rob Sved

Workbook authors: Fiona Beddall and Teresa Bestwick

Course Consultants: Elaine Boyd and Paul Dummett

Publisher: Sherrise Roehr
Executive Editor: Siân Mavor
Publishing Consultant: Karen Spiller
Editorial Project Manager: Laura Brant
Director of Global Marketing: Ian Martin
Heads of Regional Marketing:
Charlotte Ellis (Europe, Middle East, and Africa)
Kiel Hamm (Asia)
Irina Pereyra (Latin America)
Product Marketing Manager: Dave Spain
Senior Content Project Manager: Nick Ventullo
Media Researcher: Leila Hishmeh
Art Director: Brenda Carmichael
Operations Coordinator: Hayley Chwazik-Gee
Manufacturing Buyer: Elaine Bevan
Composition: emc design ltd.



ISBN: 978-1-337-79772-6

**National Geographic Learning**
Cheriton House, North Way,
Andover, Hampshire, SP10 5BE
United Kingdom

Locate your local office at **international.cengage.com/region**

Visit National Geographic Learning online at **ELTNGL.com**
Visit our corporate website at **www.cengage.com**

Printed in Greece by Bakis SA
Print Number: 01 Print Year: 2019